Adult Children of Borderline Parents

(2 Books in 1)

The Complete Guide to Understanding BPD and Staying Mentally Tough

Linda Hill

Table of Contents

Book #1

Borderline Personality Disorder

How to Communicate and Support Loved Ones With BPD. Skills to Manage Intense Emotions & Improve Your Relationship

INTRODUCTION

Shattering the Mystery of BPD

You look at me and cry, "Everything hurts". I hold you and whisper, "But everything can heal."

–Rupi Kaur

There are two huge misconceptions about Borderline Personality Disorder (BPD) that prevent many people from seeking help when they feel they don't fit into their world the way society says they should. The first is that this is just another branch off the personality disorder tree, relating to toxic or abusive relationships. The other is the stigma that's still placed on mental illness, especially when the condition is a more serious diagnosis. That stigma needs to be shattered, for both the person living with BPD as well as everyone who loves them.

As you'll realize, if you haven't already, BPD is less about an inappropriate personality, and more about being able to control moods and the responses to stressors that trigger those moods. The best place for those who want to help these individuals should begin with having a solid understanding of how most of us handle the usual ups and downs we face in life. For most of us, stress is a natural part of life that we learn to cope with as best as we can. We know that things don't always pan out the way they're planned, and we adapt to surprises, changes, or blips in those plans as best as we can. BPD interferes with this logical process.

Individuals with BPD don't see that gray area most of the rest of us do. We learn at an early age that not everything is black and white. We learn that there is a life beyond our own, and that not everything going on is related to us. Living life based on those black and white extremes is what elicits much of the disappointment BPD sufferers feel.

For example, if a friend doesn't respond immediately to a text message, there could be many reasons for that: Their phone is shut off, they didn't hear/see the notification, they don't have their phone with them, they're going through something themselves requiring their attention at that moment, etc. These things make sense to us, and we know that person will get back to us eventually. For a person living with BPD, however, they'd think more along the lines of: They don't like me. They're ignoring me. I'm unlovable. I don't deserve friends. For those of us who love a person with BPD, *this* is how they see the world. In order to help them, we need to put ourselves beside them within those extremes that are very real to them. Only then can we guide them to a different way of seeing the world.

A person living with BPD is aware of what's happening inside of them, they just don't understand *why* they do the things they do. If they were able to make that connection, they'd be able to reach out to us before turning to maladaptive ways of coping. Probably the most painful part of this condition, for those of us on the outside looking in, is that they truly don't understand why those around them won't give up on them. If they believe they aren't worth saving, that nothing will help them no matter what options are there, why do we keep trying to help them? Why don't we just give up on them? They don't believe they can be 'fixed,' so why would we keep trying to?

Above everything else, those who love a person with BPD absolutely need to take one point to heart: We don't *fix* people; we *heal* them. People aren't machines that simply need a tweak here or there in order to function properly. People need unconditional love, understanding, support, and guidance. They need the assurance that no matter what they do, say, choose, or how hard they try pushing us away, we will be there. They need to know they aren't defined by any wrong turn they make any more than they're defined by their condition. At least that's how it should be.

It is, at times, an excruciating thing for supporters of individuals with this disorder to walk alongside them, giving their support to a person who may seem not to even want it. Their words will cut deeply, their actions will seem unwarranted and hurtful, and their attempts at keeping us at arms length so we'll give up, make us question, at times, why we don't walk away. We can't. We won't. Because we know that deep down inside of them, they need us. Maybe not today, or even tomorrow, but the light will go on. And when it does, they'll see we're there and always have been.

The purpose of this book isn't just to arm supporters with knowledge about BPD, and how it affects sufferers. Its other purpose is to support the supporters in seeing the world through the sufferer's eyes. Maybe from that view they'll have some comfort in knowing they aren't alone in their daily battle with a condition they can't see, but know is trying to control their loved one. We may not be able to remove the disorder itself, but we can help our loved one take their power back and be all they're meant to be.

CHAPTER 1

Understanding BPD

One small crack does not mean that you are broken. It means that you were put to the test and you didn't fall apart.

–Linda Poindexter

There are times when we feel that all efforts we make to help someone with a mental or psychological condition are lost. Whether it's an acquaintance, a friend, relative, or significant other, one of the worst feelings is when we *know* something is hurting that person, but have no idea how to save them. We're literally standing by as they're constantly fighting with something that can't be seen, heard, or felt, but it's very real.

The main focus of this chapter is to help those close to a person with BPD understand the condition a little better. We can't possibly know what they are truly feeling, or why they do the things that they do. What having this knowledge and level of understanding *does* give us is the ability to see how the world may look and feel through their eyes. Having this enables us to think before reacting or responding so that our words or actions *help* rather than *escalate*.

Those who have been a strong supporter of a person with BPD may already be aware of some of this information, but it's always better to have more than to not have enough. We'll start with detailing exactly what BPD is, the specific signs/causes, and when to recognize when something is beyond "intense sadness" or "acting out," and strong indications something is truly wrong that requires professional intervention.

Finally, we'll give suggestions on how to be able to tell the difference between BPD and other personality disorders or other conditions with similar symptoms (e.g., bipolar disorder).

No matter how small a supporter may think a sign is initially, it could help with making sure the sufferer is being guided to the best possible path to coping with their condition. It's important to remember that there isn't a 'quick fix' in helping a loved one with BPD. It will take time and a strong sense of knowing that there will be days with great success, and others where many steps are taken backwards. It's all par for the course, and there will be a time when some strategy, or therapeutic method, will finally click. Until that time comes, be as supportive, perseverant, and ever-present as you can be.

They'll remember that above all else.

BPD 101: What It Is, What It Isn't, and How to 'See' It, Even When It's Hidden

Although it's not considered a 'newly' diagnosed condition, BPD is relatively new to the field of research. It's been a puzzling condition to both differentiate from conditions with similar symptoms, as well as to be seen as a stand alone condition with its own diagnostic procedures, causes, treatment, and prognosis. Even part of the clinical term ('borderline') has been the platform of debate.

Initially, this condition was viewed as a 'borderline' between psychosis and neurosis, which wasn't really accurate. Plus, the term doesn't describe the condition well, leaving others to believe sufferers merely have a problem with their personality that can be tweaked, rather than a debilitating condition that interferes with a person's ability to function. That's the base of a great deal of misjudgment and prejudice leading society to forget that BPD is a clinical diagnosis, not a definition of the individual.

Today, there is more focus on a sufferer's inability to self-regulate, as well as their struggles with their emotions, cognitive thinking, behaviors, relationships, and self-image.

While learning about this confusing disorder, one way to look at it from the sufferer's point of view is by thinking of it as having nerve endings that are constantly exposed and vulnerable. That would make a person much more sensitive to everything, right? Being that sensitive would tend to make a person highly reactive, even if the trigger didn't seem major to the average viewer (that would equal an internal nuclear war to the sufferer). Not being able to shield those exposed nerve endings can result in the inability to calm down that leads to aggressiveness, inconsolable responses, and finding maladaptive, impulsive, or even dangerous, ways to adapt. *That* is the side of BPD that supporters, or people completely unaware of the condition, see.

A person going through these intense thoughts and emotions aren't even able to tell us what's going on inside of them because they aren't in touch enough with themselves enough to explain to others what's in their head. Their self-image, even what they like or don't, are confusing and questionable to them. They doubt everything and everyone, and trust? In simplest terms, they don't.

We'll go over nine of the most common signs in BPD sufferers. Each person living with this condition will experience different combinations of the following, and even at different levels of intensity, but for the most part these become obvious:

1. **Untrusting.** Individuals with BPD often misinterpret others' motives. They don't trust their own thoughts or motives, so when another person does or says something that isn't in line with their own line of thoughts, they often have feelings of suspicion. In worst case scenarios, they may even experience *dissociation* where they'll literally disconnect with their self-identity.

2. **Abandonment anxiety.** This is a significant sign and a very common trigger for many BPD sufferers. They fear being left alone or abandoned so much that something as small as not getting an immediate response from a text, or as

impacting as a loved one being late coming home is enough to catapult them into a panicked state.

3. **Volcanic anger.** These individuals have explosive anger and short fuses. It doesn't take much to set them off. They'll yell, throw things, and seem inconsolable in their anger, but they rarely take it out on others. Most times, their anger is internal and stemming from their negative feelings toward themselves. And there are moments when their anger comes fast, hard, and out of nowhere.

4. **Unhealthy relationships.** These individuals tend to gravitate to relationships that are intense, short-lived, and emphasize their insatiable feelings of unworthiness. They may even try believing what they feel is true love, only to be left with disappointment, and self-hatred. For them, relationships are either perfect or awful with no middle ground. This extends to friendships, family or other close relations where the other person often feels they're spinning just trying to understand what's expected of them.

5. **Emptiness.** This is one of the more heartbreaking, and hardest to understand, symptoms. These individuals have an unfillable hole, leaving them in a constant state of feeling like 'nothing' or life is 'meaningless.' They try filling this void with food, substances, sex, or other temporary satisfaction often making them feel even worse. From a loved one's view, it's so upsetting because it feels that all attempts of trying to make the sufferer happy in some way, nothing seems to work.

6. **Uncertain self-image.** When a person doesn't connect with their inner self or identity, they can't be stable with their self-image. They can go from sky-high confidence (leaning to the side of arrogance), crashing to self-hatred—sometimes within a few minutes. This uncertainty about the self results in an unclear idea of who they are, or where they want their life to go. This causes them to change friends, jobs, lovers, ethics, values or even their sexuality.

7. **Harmful behavior.** Self-harm, impulsiveness, and behaviors that put the sufferer in risky situations is not unusual. From an outside view, this can be seen with shoplifting, eating disorders, risky sexual encounters, or substance abuse. Basically, anything the BPD sufferer does in this mindset is excessive and with no regard for personal safety.

8. **Self-harm.** We've pulled this one out as a separate point because the practice can be seen in most cases of BPD. Although this group is high-risk for attempting suicide, self-harm is the act of hurting oneself without the intent of dying. It can be seen as cutting, burning, purging, choking oneself, etc. Even behaviors such as piercing or tattooing can be taken to this point.

9. **Mood swings.** This is one of the base components of this condition, and a main symptom shared with similar conditions (e.g., bipolar disorder). Extreme and unstable swings are in mood intense and happen often, but do tend taper off as quickly as they come on.

These are some of the main signs, but several of them are listed in other conditions. So in order to ensure that a correct diagnosis is given, there also needs to be a solid understanding of what BPD isn't.

What BPD Isn't

There are several frustrations both for those who love a person with BPD, and for those who are diagnosed with it. One is that there is no biological test that can distinguish one mental or psychological condition from another. Another is that BPD is one of the most misdiagnosed conditions. So much so that there's no accurate prevalence of the condition except an estimate that between 2% and 6% of the population have BPD (*NAMI*, 2017). If this is true, it shows prevalence warranting more research. So why, then, is this condition so highly misdiagnosed?

Here are a few possible reasons:

- **Misunderstanding about the base of BPD.** Not understanding the difference between *mood* disorders and *personality* disorders. The former category involves conditions where individuals display severe and rapid changes in mood. The latter involves conditions focusing on irregular ways of thinking, feeling, and behaving that are different from the social norm which results in distress and ability to function.

- **Social and professional stigmas.** There is a tremendous amount of stigma attached to a BPD diagnosis, not just with society but even among mental health professionals. In fact, this stigma can do more harm to individuals and their loved ones who just want answers. To make this point clearer, the base of stigma is judgement, blame, and discrimination. These are all worry points for a person who lives with BPD, making them feel even more ashamed leading them to try hiding their condition even more deeply. Repressing or hiding their condition leads to even more severe emotional dysregulation and attempts with dangerous ways of coping. Plus, there are many mental health professionals who won't diagnose a person with BPD as the label tends to stick with them throughout their lifetime.

- **BPD isn't treated as a whole condition.** As mentioned earlier, there are many other conditions that have the same symptoms as BPD, and a person with BPD can also have these conditions as part of their overall diagnosis. When professionals focus more on the individual conditions, rather than treating BPD as a whole condition, the sufferer may not be receiving the treatment specialized to their disorder.

- **BPD isn't gender-specific.** This is an important point. Women, by nature of their gender, are often highly misdiagnosed with mood-related disorders, while men are often undiagnosed. This should be a concern for those trying to get to the bottom of their or loved one's mental health issues. In these modern times, one's gender alone should not be a deciding factor in diagnosing BPD or any mood disorder.

- **BPD isn't age-specific.** There are many professionals who see BPD in youth, but hesitate in stamping a teen or young adult with such a heavy diagnosis. The concern is that the stigma of the disorder will follow the youth into adult life, resulting in being unfairly discriminated against. This hesitation prevents many youth from receiving proper treatment, which could prepare them better for coping with their condition down the road. The earlier it's detected, the higher the changes the youth has of becoming a productive adult.

There are many other factors that may interfere with obtaining a proper diagnosis, and it's the lack of understanding that prevents many people from getting the help they need. The more families and loved ones of sufferers educate themselves with these issues, the better they'll be able to advocate for getting the right diagnosis and treatment.

Distinguishing Among the Four Types of BPD

In our next chapter, we'll be going through the diagnostic process for BPD. It may be valuable for those going with a loved one along this difficult road to be armed with information ahead of time. There will be a great deal of jargon, diagnostic terms, and other things that may not be easy to understand. The whole process may be easier to digest when the person being analyzed, as well as those by their side, have some knowledge behind them. Family members and loved ones need to remember that they know the sufferer better than anyone else, which makes them an expert and a valuable part of the treatment team.

There are four main categories of BPD, although an individual can be set under more than one or different ones along their treatment journey. For the sake of our discussion, we'll separate them so that family members and/or loved ones can ask questions or raise concerns certain symptoms may not be known or seen.

1. **Impulsive.** The focus of those under this category is their impulsiveness, often expressed in dangerous ways. Their actions are often carried out with no regard for their personal safety, for the feelings of others and with no concern of consequences for their behavior. Those with this type of BPD are often charismatic, energetic, detached, flirtatious, and motivated by what they want. Their displayed behaviors may include:

   a. binging—eating, spending, hoarding

   b. risky/self-destructive actions—unprotected sex, multiple sex partners, consuming substances excessively, driving while impaired, befriending individuals actively participating in risky behavior, or gambling

   c. aggression—angry outbursts, physical fighting, breaking/throwing/hitting things, or yelling fits

2. **Discouraged.** This is also termed "quiet BPD" because a lot of their symptoms are directed to themselves and hidden. They have an intense fear of being alone or being abandoned, often taking extreme measures to ensure they aren't. They keep their emotions deeply buried, and lay blame on themselves even if it's unwarranted. They are clingy, needy, codependent, and inconsolably moody when abandonment fears are triggered. Individuals in this category are also known to:

   a. be perfectionists

   b. feel detached in large groups

   c. disbelieve they have strong connections with others

   d. seek approval but also isolate

   e. self-harm or experience continued suicidal thoughts

   f. suffer feelings of continued loneliness or emptiness

g. be successful or high-functioning

3. **Self-destructive.** Individuals in this category are consumed with self-hatred and bitterness. Those in this category display many symptoms similar to bipolar disorder. Symptoms such as restlessness, abnormally high energy level, feelings of euphoria, and decreased desire for sleep could be mistaken as mania, so loved ones need to be able to distinguish between mania and this form of BPD. Those in this category often display:

   a. substance abuse—alcohol, recreational drugs, over-the-counter and prescription medications

   b. risky, adrenaline-inducing behavior—the concern is less on the activity itself and more on the person jumping in impulsively without thinking

   c. self-harm—cutting, burning, choking, scratching, hitting, pulling out hair, etc.

4. **Petulant.** Individuals in this category may seem angry one moment, then inconsolable the next. Their mood swings are huge, intense, and unpredictable. Those in this category believe they are unloved and unworthy, which leads to them having challenges in relationships. Their unhealthy need for control is fed by their manipulative nature, and they often resort to maladaptive ways of coping with their discomfort. Petulant sufferers can be seen as:

   a. irritable and impatient

   b. stubborn and defiant

   c. passive-aggressive

   d. having severe mood swings

Above all else, people within each of these categories experience a tremendous amount of emotional pain, which they may not even understand themselves. These different categories show how two people with BPD will experience the condition very differently, and one person can experience it in many different ways.

This may shed some light on how supporters may feel lost with their efforts in trying to help. Rest assured that even though the sufferer may seem different from one day to the next, or even one moment to the next, it's important to show ongoing and unconditional love and support in any scenario. It matters, even if they don't have the words to say so.

Things That People With BPD Want Us to Know

BPD is a scary condition to live with, and even scarier to watch. For those of us on the outside looking in, as hard as we try we can't possibly understand what's going on underneath. They push us away not because they don't want us there, but because they don't know how to make us see the world the way they do. And rather than allowing us in, they tell us to stop trying to help. Of course, we aren't just going to turn away.

In addition to arming ourselves with knowledge before venturing down that diagnosis and treatment road, it may also be helpful for supporters to bring how their loved one with BPD may be feeling. Here are a few insightful points, important to shed light on in an initial intervention meeting:

- **We're scared you'll leave us, even if things are okay.** Their deep-felt fear of abandonment is there even when a relationship seems to be going well. They're afraid they'll do something wrong, that they don't deserve us, and legitimately wonder why we stay by their side. This makes them seem 'needy' or 'clingy,' and it may be hard to deal with, but it stems from a real fear they have.

- **Life is emotionally painful, like living with untreated burns.** Imagine how difficult life could be if we had no control of our emotions or our responses. How difficult would it be to explain how we could be elated one moment, then minutes later be inconsolable and have no idea how we got there? *That* torment is how

BPD feels, and they come across as 'over-sensitive' when they have no control over those things.

- **I feel everything to the extreme.** As touched on earlier, there is no middle ground for those with BPD. You're either sky high, or lower than low, and there's no in between. This part of the condition is exhausting not only for them, but for every person around them. But in their mind it's 'normal,' and they are confused or even hurt when we react negatively.

- **I don't have multiple personalities.** This point is added in here to show why, sometimes, BPD is misdiagnosed. A person with this condition doesn't have more than one personality. They have a disorder that affects how they're able to regulate their emotions, thought patterns, and behavior, and may withdraw when feeling low, but this is not an indication of having other personalities.

- **I don't mean to be manipulative, and I'm not dangerous to you.** To clarify, not all BPD sufferers are manipulative or dangerous. When they are manipulative, it isn't with malicious intent. Most times it's to try convincing others they're doing better than we believe them to be. And they are rarely dangerous to anyone. In fact, the only person they're in danger to is themselves.

- **Treatment is exhausting, disappointing, and frustrating.** We'll be going further into this point in a later chapter but, we need to be empathetic on this. We as supporters move with our loved one from one form of therapy or treatment to another, and don't always see the results we hope for. Think of how a person with BPD must feel in that situation? For an individual who already has little or no hope, trying one treatment after another with no real improvement can often make them feel they're 'unfixable.' One response to this that we'll go back to every so often in our discussions is: We don't 'fix' people; we help heal them.

- **I want so much to be loved, I just don't always know how to.** Individuals have so much love in them. So much so it can often feel smothering and overwhelming. Although it can be difficult to have a relationship with them, all they want is to know their feelings are returned, and that we won't leave them.

As you move forward into the diagnostic and therapeutic step, remember that by gaining a compassionate understanding perspective of BPD, and how it affects our loved one, you are doing everything you can.

And they know.

CHAPTER 2

The Diagnostic Process

Mental health problems don't define who you are. They are something you experience. You walk in the rain and you feel the rain, but, importantly, you are not the rain.

–Matt Haig

Those of us who have tried the best we could to help our loved one through all the ups, downs, fits, rage, threats of harm and suicide get to a crossroads. One path confirms all we've been told from everyone around us who don't see this person the way we have. Those are the ones who tell us our struggling loved one is 'fine' and that they are just 'eccentric' or in a stage. Discounting what our gut has been telling us for a long time. The other path is the handful of people who confirm what our gut has been telling us. They know our loved one isn't 'fine,' 'eccentric,' or in a stage they'll grow out of. And that's the path we have to follow to get help. But it won't be an easy one.

Of course, there is the positive aspect of finally having a name for the unseen thing that has been controlling our loved one every waking moment. It's a relief to most supporters to have an explanation for everything their loved one has been through, and hope it will be the first step in getting effective treatment.

This chapter focuses on the diagnostic process from getting a referral all the up to figuring out the best form of treatment and/or therapy, and everything in between. It can be a long, frustrating, and turbulent time, especially if a loved one isn't able to get in to see an expert right away. We're also going to describe the process, including who will be on the mental health team. We'll also expand on points made in the last chapter on why BPD is difficult to distinguish from other conditions with similar symptoms, even though it's known to be treated for more than one mental health or psychological condition simultaneously.

Finally, we'll be closing the chapter with a special section on BPD in young people, and some more ways to view the condition through the eyes of the sufferer. We want to create the most complete picture of BPD possible because the more we understand the whole of who they are, the more trust they'll have in us to help them.

How BPD Is Diagnosed

When a person is physically ill, and is able to identify specific symptoms they can share with their primary healthcare provider, digging for the cause of the illness can be found relatively easily. There are many answers in our blood, for example, so a thorough series of bloodwork will enable the physician to follow a path to pin down the cause. For a person who has more internal illness concerns, the path isn't as clearly set.

There is no blood test that detects a mental or psychological concern, such as BPD. There are no scans, X-rays, ultrasounds, or any other sort of procedure that would help a doctor figure out what is causing an individual to think and behave the way they do. There may be certain MRI tests that can eliminate specific health issues, such as tumors, but that's a reach at best. This is a major concern for any of us wanting answers for our loved one, and why we feel anger and frustration with not knowing where to turn.

It can be a lengthy process because all there is to go from initially are the behavioral symptoms that can be seen, and the cognitive symptoms that are overtly coped with (e.g., self-harm). It's discouraging as a supporter or loved one to feel there's nothing that can be done until the affected person either reaches out to us, which rarely happens, or hurts themselves to the point of hospitalization. These shouldn't be our only options., which is why we'll share suggestions on how to maneuver through the right channels to get a loved one into the hands of the person who'll be able to help them.

Let's start with discussing the professional path who are the main players on the BPD diagnostic team:

- **Primary healthcare provider.** Whether this is a traditional doctor, naturopath or other sort of health professional, this is usually the person to get the ball rolling. Normally in order to see a mental health specialist, there needs to be a referral from the GP or family physician. This is based on symptom concerns or any sort of visible self-harm, or even if the person has a history of depression or anxiety. The problem is that it can be a long wait to see a specialist, and in many situations this isn't feasible. In these situations, it's wise to have a person who can see the sufferer until there's an opening with a specialist.

- **Psychologist.** There are many psychologists who work through clinics or physician's offices where a person can get immediate help while waiting to be seen by a psychiatrist. Supporters should make it clear with the physician that the psychologist should have experience working with individuals who have the exact symptoms the sufferer displays or, even better, a person who has direct experience working with individuals who have serious mental health concerns. It's important that the person with BPD feels safe and has a connection with who they'll be seeing, and that person should be available to see the sufferer regularly. Avoiding the possibility of feeding the individual's fear of abandonment needs to be in the open from the start.

- **Nutritionist.** This isn't always necessary but if the sufferer is practicing self-harm in the form of purging or other sort of eating disorder, this individual needs to be a part of the team. A brain that is nourished is in a healthier place to accept other forms of intervention that will happen.

- **Drug/alcohol counselor.** Again, not every individual with BPD will turn to substances to ease their symptoms but a large portion of them do. In that case, if the psychologist doesn't have specific experience in this area, it would be a good idea to have the physician recommend a person who's an expert in eliciting healthier ways of coping.

- **Psychiatrist.** It can take up to a year or longer to get in to see a psychiatrist, especially one who specializes in conditions such as BPD. This person would be considered the head of the team since they decide the procedures that can be tried as well as any sort of medicinal approaches that may ease symptoms. They have authority to prescribe medications and, usually, have access to a wider options of treatment than psychologists do.

In the case of younger individuals, other members of the mental health team might be school counselors as the connection to the person's needs in school, as well as a connection with Child and Family Services in the case of any family issues contributing to triggers.

After an assessment of the symptoms the person has—there need to be at least five out of the nine symptoms discussed in the first chapter—there are usually discussions with family to get a history as well as to get a full picture of what others close to the sufferer have noticed. The individual will also have to go into detail regarding their symptoms including which ones are most debilitating and how they interfere with everyday living. That may be the hardest part because those living with BPD aren't always able to express what they're feeling or have connections with what they're experiencing.

What can we do, as supporters, to make sure that the mental health team has everything they need to put together the best therapeutic plan? We know firsthand that a person with BPD isn't always upfront with what they're going through, nor will their trust issues allow them to be honest that they're struggling to others. Be rest assured that these experts know exactly what individuals with BPD will do, and they know what to watch for.

Here are a few common things that people with BPD will say or do when they need help, but don't come right out to say so. These can be added to the list brought to the mental health team, so they know what to expect when working with the sufferer:

- **I'm fine.** Most of us say these words when we don't want to talk. It's the fastest way to say, "I'm really not fine, but I don't want to talk about it right now." For a person with BPD, this can't be an acceptable response because when they aren't encouraged to talk about it, they're already past the point of being okay and moving into a total meltdown phase. Let the team know if this is a typical response and to leave it with that response.

- **I'm overwhelmed.** This isn't one that we'll hear many people say, especially younger sufferers, because admitting this means they aren't in control, or close to falling apart. But if they're brave enough to say so, immediate intervention is needed.

- **Maybe I'm supposed to be alone.** This is the all-or-nothing perspective leaking out. The usual tactic here is to be told that they aren't meant to be alone, and that they'll still have us. Remember that their abandonment fear comes across as them pushing us away, but it's almost like being tested that we won't leave.

- **I don't feel good.** This is a simpler way of saying that things are brewing inside of them and if they don't have a safe way of releasing it, they'll explode. Those who aren't as versed with BPD may think this is hinting at something more physically wrong, but it's much deeper than that.

- **I don't know.** When asked what's wrong, this is a very typical response. What's important to remember is that they have so many emotions and thoughts going on, they may truly not know what exactly is wrong. How can they explain to us what's wrong if they don't know themselves?

- **I'm sorry.** Those with BPD apologize often, even when they have nothing to apologize for. When we look at them closely, we'll see that they are literally terrified of everything: their feelings, disappointing us, being a burden, or even their own minds. They need to know they don't need to be sorry for what's happening inside of them, and we aren't going anywhere.

- **I'm going to bed.** Sometimes when the world is too much to handle, they think that the best thing for them is to shut the world out by going to sleep. What they really need is to be distracted from their thoughts. As supporters, we know that in that frame of mind leaving them alone with their thoughts is a dangerous thing.

- **I just have a headache.** Quite often, individuals with BPD will say this to us when we notice a change in their mood, when they aren't very responsive, or when they "space out." This is also an excuse to go lay down. It's a beginning sign that the person is struggling. Supporters should bring up to the mental health team if they ever noticed the sufferer asks for pain medication when indicating they have a headache. If the person practices self-harm regularly, it could be indicative of hiding pills for future use.

- **Do you want to hang out?** This is a way the person with BPD lets us subtly know they don't want to be alone. If they come to us every day, or a few times throughout the day, they're asking for help in their way.

- **I don't feel right/I feel weird.** This is a cry for help meaning that the person doesn't feel safe with their thoughts to the point that they're disassociating. The way their emotions or thoughts make their body respond feels strange and uncomfortable. They are asking not to be alone.

- **Saying 'okay' or giving a thumb's up.** Usually they do this not to worry those around them, when they don't have the energy or brain space to say more than that, or just to get us to back off a bit.

- **I've just been busy.** An individual with BPD doesn't want to let others know they've been avoiding social scenes, or isolating to not face others, so they lie. It's better, in their mind, to say they've been too busy to stay in touch rather than that they've intentionally been avoiding people.

- **I hate you/get out/leave me alone.** As hurtful as it is to hear these words, it's important that we remember that this isn't what our loved one wants to say. They really don't want us to leave, but they're riddled with guilt, shame, frustration, or whatever they may be feeling at that moment, and those are the words that come out rather than, "Can you just sit with me for a minute?"

Even though it's a great idea to share with the mental health team that the sufferer uses any of these phrases regularly, they've probably had a few of them fired their way too. Anything you share with the team, no matter how insignificant it may seem, is a step closer to creating the best possible therapeutic path for the sufferer.

Throughout the diagnosis process, remember that the team is careful when administering a BPD diagnosis because there are several other conditions that have similar symptoms, and in order for treatment to be as effective as possible the diagnosis must be accurate. A person can have other diagnoses with a BPD one (e.g., depression, anxiety, PTSD, etc.), but each is a separate condition that needs to be treated individually.

Things We Shouldn't Do With A Person with BPD

We've dealt with our loved one with BPD for awhile, and have tried helping them cope as best as we can. As soon as we are able to move our loved one onto the therapeutic path, we discover that some of the tactics we've tried, just to make things go a little more smoothly, may not have been the best strategies. The mental health team will guide you to tweak ones that worked, or to remove others that unintentionally accelerated the situation at hand.

Even experts in BPD will miss signs or clues because even though sufferers may not understand their condition, they do know how people respond to the things they say and do. Unfortunately, there's a lot of room for misunderstanding and miscommunication when being close to a person with this condition. It's hurtful to know we've been lied to, mistreated, or manipulated by the person we are simply trying to help. But we'd never just give up on them.

The mental health team is made up of people who are experts in the condition itself; family, friends, or loved ones are the experts in day-to-day life with the person affected by it. While waiting for our therapy plan, the top priority is to acknowledge that boundaries need to be set and stay firmly maintained. These boundaries help establish rules to avoid or distinguish confrontations, arguments, or misunderstandings more quickly. And they also help to prevent any maladaptive actions to be absorbed into routine, making it much more difficult to change.

That all being said, when establishing these boundaries, supporters should *not*:

- **Feed into neediness for attention**. Not all individuals with bpd want or seek attention, but some do. It's usually seen as bringing in another person into an argument (e.g., *triangulation*), receiving validation for things they shouldn't be doing, or trying to get a rise out of us. The best way not to feed into this behavior is minimizing our own reactions, and not allowing others not directly involved in a situation to add to the chaos.

- **Normalize behavior or minimize our intuition.** As human beings, we all experience intense emotions periodically that affect our behavior. We all get angry, and we've all had moments where we've overreacted. But when the behaviors are intense and happen often, the behavior needs to be addressed. When things seem truly wrong, they usually are, and normalizing or minimizing it won't help.

- **Get pulled into the drama.** As an extension of the point on triangulation, we shouldn't allow ourselves to be drawn into the middle of a situation. To avoid this from happening, don't discuss a situation with anyone outside of the situation.

- **Believe that they'll "get over it" or "snap out of it."** Those of us who've dealt with our loved one long enough already know these are not feasible thoughts. Individuals with bpd aren't able to just "snap out of" a mindset they get into because they don't have the tools to cope effectively yet. Don't be told, or allow others to think, this is a possibility.

- **Normalize any sort of harmful or risky behavior.** This is a tough one because individuals with bpd aren't always candid with their behavior. For example, finding out that they didn't 'just go for coffee' with a friend, but were actually having a sexual encounter with a random partner. It may be difficult to accept that the sufferer in our life is engaging in high-risk behavior or seeking stimulation in ways that are unhealthy and dangerous. This will continue if their actions are normalized in any way.

- **Be made to feel deeply hurt by impulsive remarks.** Many individuals with bpd struggle with deep anger management and impulsivity. Regardless of all they're going through, they shouldn't be allowed to disrespect or devalue those close to them. In such cases, the person needs to be called out for such treatment and have the boundaries re-established. If the treatment continues, supporters should distance themselves until the boundaries are respected again.

- **Be drawn into the sufferer's abandonment fears.** A person with bpd has difficulty with making relationships work because they either push the individual away when they get too close to avoid any anxiety, or the sufferer bombards the person with needs for attention and companionship. One has to be careful with how they empathize with a person who has bpd who has these strong fears of abandonment. It's possible to be supportive without inadvertently enabling.

- **Be emotional 'prey.'** this is difficult for a supporter to see clearly when their heartfelt intention is simply to be there. An example here would be the sufferer asking for money or to have things bought for them, then don't need the supporter after that. This is another area where those boundaries need to be set up.

- **Allow undesirable behavior to become habitual or routine.** This point also falls in line with being emotionally guilted into agreeing to things that the sufferer will make routine. Some examples might be eating alone in their room (especially if they have an eating disorder), being on their device past the time or duration allowance, or going/staying out past curfew. Once an undesirable behavior becomes routine, it's much harder to have rules respected or to reset the boundary.

- **Be the main 'go to' person all the time.** It's a wonderful feeling to be the one the bpd sufferer turns to when things are too much for them. But it also means that their 'go to' would also be the one they manipulate the most or treat the worst because, in their head, they know we'll stay no matter how negatively we're treated.

- **Respond to their attempts at control or manipulation.** To respond emotionally to any sort of ill-treatment the sufferer attempts gives them leeway in believing they have control over us. The less we respond to their actions, the less likely they'll keep trying.

- **Be manipulated into their harmful cycles.** This is also a tough point because we always want to be there. There are times that are triggers for the bpd sufferer such as birthdays, holidays, summertime, etc. These are those times when they display symptoms, but they'll also try getting what they want from us using those painful times for them to get it. We need to be strong enough to call the person out, and remind them you're there to help them in ways you can but it isn't fair that they draw us into their pain cycle.

- **Participate in codependency.** We absolutely want to help and to be a strong presence in their lives, but there's a fine line between being unconditionally supportive and empathetic, and being codependent. The former shows we're there for them, but will not allow them to be codependent. Even with a condition like bpd, the person needs to take accountability for their actions. We aren't responsible for their choices, they are.

With these points laid out, it's easier to see that even though we're by their side through their diagnosis and treatment path, we can still do more harm than good if we aren't in tune with the person and know when they truly need our help or when we're enabling them. Once in therapy, the mental health team can offer valuable strategies to make us aware of these attempts and the best way to ward them off.

BPD vs Bipolar Disorder

Ever since BPD was included in the Diagnostic and Statistical Manual of Mental Disorders (DSM-MD) in 1980, it's been the focus of controversy. The main reason for this is because there still hasn't been a resolution to whether or not it's related to bipolar disorder as the two disorders share so many similar symptoms. Although there are similarities, there are also different symptoms specific to each disorder that distinguish them as separate.

Similarities

The main reason there are experts who believe that BPD and bipolar disorder are related is because they both focus on mood instability and extreme impulsivity. Those with bipolar experience high mood swings between mania and depression. In a manic state, they have a decreased need for sleep and are active, often taking on many tasks at once. These severe changes in mood can last weeks or months at a time at each point.

Those with BPD also experience mood swings, emotional dysregulation, and instability. The moves from one extreme to the other can be within minutes at times, but don't last as long as what's seen in bipolar individuals.

Differences

With the similarities, there are major differences that separate the two disorders:

- The quality of the mood disorders differs. For bipolar individuals, the moods go from elated highs (mania) to extreme lows (depression). Those with BPD are in a constant state of emotional pain, feelings of emptiness, panic, anger, hopelessness, and loneliness.

- Changes in mood for those with BPD usually occur after an environmental trigger, where a person with bipolar's mood changes often seem to come from nowhere and not usually not triggered.

- Those with BPD rarely experience feelings of elation. Normally, they go from feeling upset to 'okay.' Bipolar is either devastatingly low, or extremely elated.

There is continued research being done on BPD, but there hasn't been enough proven evidence so far that the two are related. It's important for supporters to make sure to advise the mental health team of any family history of either, or both, disorders so a more accurate diagnosis can be given.

The main concern is that because both of these conditions require medication, at least focusing on the mood regulation, a misdiagnosis would also mean incorrect administration of medications. For example, someone with bipolar needs to be treated for *both* mania and depression requiring specific medicinal regimen. For a person with BPD, there isn't a specific medication to treat it beyond antidepressants and mood regulators. Administering either condition with the wrong medications could have detrimental effects, so making sure the diagnosis is absolute is vital.

If nothing else, having this information may guide supporters through the diagnosis with less turbulence. There will be days when what the mental health team tells us has question marks all over it. Sufferers should never be intimidated to ask questions, bring information of their own to the table, or even share any concerns regarding the diagnosed condition.

In the end, every person wants the same thing. We all want what's best for the sufferer, and for them to finally reach a level of happiness they deserve to feel.

CHAPTER 3

Treating a Person With BPD

I understand your pain. Trust me, I do. I've seen people go from the darkest moments in their lives to living a happy, fulfilling life. You can do it too. I believe in you. You are not a burden. You will* never *be a burden.

—Sophie Turner

The diagnostic process was difficult, but the positive that came from it was finally having a name for what's been plaguing your loved one. There's an explanation for their intense behavior, and now there's something to research further. Being aware of a condition fills us with hope that we can finally do something to help our loved one. Don't lose that hope, because it will help us move the individual forward no matter what hurdles pop up along the path to healing.

There are several options available for treating a person with BPD, and what works in one person's situation may not be helpful at all to another. That's why it's so important to work with the mental health team in finding the "right fit." It will take time to find the right treatment plan that helps to ease symptoms, rather than escalating them. This means trying different strategies, or the combination of several, until something clicks. It can be a difficult process for both the sufferer as well as those of us who just want the individual not to hurt anymore.

It's important for those supporting a loved one with BPD to keep two things in mind. First, the situation will seem worse before it gets better. It's similar to healing a wound that has been left untreated for too long, and has gotten infected. The infection has to be dealt with and cleared up before the wound can heal properly. This will be the most difficult part of the treatment process, but one that the individual has to go through so they can learn to self-regulate.

The second point is that individuals with BPD often fight treatment. This stems from their belief that they "can't be fixed" or they "don't deserve to live." It's the mindset that has to be changed before any treatment can be successful. People with BPD don't want to hear that everything will be okay or that they just need to stick things out, especially since many sufferers aren't future oriented. As supporters, we need to teach the individual to be there with us in the present, in the 'now,' so that they can accept what needs to be done. There are things in the past that they'll need to address, but those things have no place in the present. And the future is something to work toward, not to worry about today. Those living with BPD can't make that distinction yet, but they'll be able to as they move through treatment.

That's what we'll discuss in this chapter First, supporters are going to need strategies of their own to help their loved one. We'll cover some suggestions on moving through the ups and downs that will come up. We also want to help supporters be an effective part of the mental health team, but also be able to read signs of a possible meltdown before it happens. This scenario is often called *splitting*, and we'll share ways to see them coming as well as suggestions on how to talk the individual through it before it goes past the point of return.

From there, we'll go over a few of the common therapy methods sought when treating a person with BPD. These methods not only help the individual learn to express themselves in better ways, but they'll also learn to connect thoughts with actions and find more effective ways of self-regulating. Finally, we'll end the chapter with a discussion for those supporters who find their loved one either fights treatment, or just refuses help. As we know, we can't force the individual to accept the treatment. However, there are strategies we can try to guide them down the path.

In the end, we all have the same end goal: to help our loved one find their path to inner peace. They'll get there.

Just never give up hope.

Treating BPD: Methods, Strategies, and Guidance

The mental health team will discuss different approaches in treating an individual with BPD. There is no one set path for every person. There are different aspects that are considered before trying anything such as how long the person has been living with it, the intensity of their symptoms, past history, if there are any other conditions in addition to BPD, and the individual's reception of help. Setting a plan is one thing, but getting the individual on board with their own treatment is another thing entirely.

Before going ahead with the treatment plan, it's important for supporters to prepare themselves for the journey ahead. After all, unless the individual has been hospitalized the mental health team won't always be there when things hit the fan. We know more than any other person how stressful it can be trying to help someone with BPD, or even to know how to respond in a specific situation.

In the case of younger individuals with BPD, or those who have made suicide attempts, hospitalization is the first point of treatment. This will be discussed in greater detail in a few minutes. For now, let's go over some strategies for supporters:

- **Learn about BPD.** We've already covered the importance of learning all you can about this condition. Not only does it help us understand more about the person who is afflicted by BPD, it also gives a more omniscient view of the person. Learning about something we don't fully understand is empowering, and we'll need that down the road when advocating for our loved one.

- **Emit confidence and respect.** There's a high association between surviving childhood trauma and BPD. Not every person who goes through trauma will develop the condition, but with such a huge relation it's important for those giving support for these individuals to bear in mind they'll need to earn their trust. They have a damaged sense of safety and control not only with themselves, but with everyone in their world. To truly help them, we need to ensure that their opinions, choices, and voice matters throughout their treatment options as well as life in general. Helping them build that confidence in themselves is how they'll learn to trust others.

- **Honesty.** Their trust issues also inflate their fear of abandonment. That means while supporting those with BPD, we need to be honest in all of our interactions with them. We need to do what we say we'll do, not to make promises we can't fulfill, and never tell them what we think they want to hear. The truth may not always be easy for them to hear, but in the end they'll appreciate being told what they *need* to know.

- **Manage conflict effectively.** Most of us know that life is never a smooth ride, and conflict is inevitable when each of us has different views, thoughts, and opinions. For a person with BPD, though, conflict means we're disappointed, angry, or wanting to end the relationship. We need to do our best to stay in that gray area they can't see, and assure them that just because we may not see eye-to-eye with them on something they've said or done, it will never change our feelings for them. Focus on the behavior, not the person, so they learn that even though you don't agree with the way they behaved, you'll still be there.

- **Encouraging maintaining professional connections.** Individuals with BPD may not be receptive to therapy or professional intervention because they don't trust others, they don't believe what they're being told, and they certainly don't like being told they have to do things a different way than they're used to. But supporters should remind them that the therapists are there to give them help in ways that may be beyond our ability. We should help them to, at the very least, take what they believe is helpful from a certain source, knowing they can alter the plan as they change.

- **Remind them of their strengths.** In an upcoming discussion, we'll be sharing how to see the positives in BPD. For now, this individual is being bombarded at every turn with what's 'wrong' with them and how to intervene in every possible scenario. What they need to hear more of is what their strengths are. These abilities, strengths, and talents are reminders that there is more to them than this condition. These strengths can also be used as positive coping methods to turn to when things feel too much for them.

- **Have fun.** They're surrounded by illness, therapy, and treatment all of the time. They also need positivity and fun mixed in. Give them memories to embrace in darker times so they know their world isn't all about BPD. Make them laugh. Do activities they enjoy. Have a picnic, go for a walk, watch a good show or concert, or any other way to forget the roles of 'sufferer' and 'supporter' for just a little while. Help them create new, beautiful memories.

- **Take any hints of suicide seriously.** Those with BPD are more at risk of suicide than almost any other group. That means that any attempt, or even hint to it, must be taken seriously. They aren't doing such things for attention, and should never be ignored. The best way to handle it is to show concern for their safety, and let them know you'd be willing to stay with them until the feelings subside.

The other point is that supporters need to practice self-care. It's stressful and exhausting to care for another person, so we must take time for ourselves too. The individual with BPD is prone to think 'me time' would mean they're burdening us. This time to care for ourselves isn't rejection or avoidance. After all, if we allow ourselves to go empty and not reenergize, how can we expect to deal with the bigger issues that come up when there's nothing left to get us through?

It makes everything else we face throughout the treatment process easier to cope with.

What Are the Common Treatments for BPD?

Usually the treatments for BPD involve psychotherapy, medication, hospitalization, or a combination of these. There are also further therapeutic methods that involve loved ones or family members so that there's full support for the sufferer. Here's a look into these areas:

- **Psychotherapy**. This is the typical form of therapy in treating BPD, and is included in conjunction with the other forms of treatment. The mental health team may opt for one of the following:

    - Cognitive Behavioral Therapy (CBT): The focus of this therapy is to help individuals recognize unhealthy behavior, beliefs, or perceptions of the self and of others. It also teaches more effective ways to respond to aggressive, negative, or suicidal thoughts.

    - Dialectical Behavioral Therapy (DBT): The focus of this form of therapy helps individuals learn to recognize, be aware of, and deal with their beliefs and behaviors. It also helps people to interpret and respond more appropriately to other people's behaviors.

    - Schema-focused therapy: In a nutshell, the focus is helping people have a more positive view of themselves and the world around them.

- **Medication.** As discussed previously, there is no medication that cures BPD, but the psychiatrist on the team may prescribe medications for mood, anxiety, and/or depression to ease symptoms. Medication is used in conjunction with therapeutic methods, which can be highly successful. The downside is that some individuals experience uncomfortable side effects that can enhance, rather than calm, the symptoms they're given to relieve. The person is unusually monitored closely in order to find the medicinal/therapeutic that is most effective.

- **Hospitalization.** This is usually the starting point for some sufferers, and the last resort for others. Hospitalization is usually the path followed when there are concerns about suicide, or if there have been suicide attempts. Hospitalization is turned to as the 'stabilization' resort as the person is monitored until the right treatment path is found. There is concern with keeping people in the hospital too long, however, as the person isn't learning to cope in the real world when living in the protective atmosphere of the hospital.

Family-based therapy is available to loved ones of those being treated for BPD where they can have therapy for themselves, or join sessions with the sufferer. These give ways for all people involved in the care and support of the individual to be on the same page, and to have any questions or concerns addressed. There are programs available to youth and teens diagnosed with BPD, which vary according to their age and what is available in their communities. Finally, holistic and alternative approaches can be highly effective for those living with BPD, which we'll go into greater detail in a later chapter.

What Is 'Splitting,' and How Do I Help a Sufferer Through It?

For those supporting a person with BPD, 'splitting' is an element of the disorder that is vital to watch for. It's essentially the cry of help before things hit the fan, and there are specific signs that may have been missed, but will be easier to pick up on the further we go down the therapeutic path.

It's when the sufferer only sees people or situations as good or bad, all or nothing, and stays in that gray area we discussed earlier. Not every person with BPD 'splits,' but it is usually a trigger response to rejection, abandonment, or reminders of childhood trauma (e.g., anniversary of events). The person goes into defense mode in order to avoid the uncomfortable, painful, or anxiety-ridden emotions connected with those situations or people. The following are some signs of splitting:

- **Saying hurtful things.** Lashing out to those of us closest to the sufferer is their way of getting rid of the feelings without actually having to deal with them. It's also a way to keep us at arm's length when they feel we're getting too close for comfort. There is usually a lot of guilt involved because they don't mean to hurt us, they just don't feel safe owning the feelings themselves.

- **Jumping to conclusions.** This is when the fear of abandonment kicks in causing them to assume the worst when there may be a logical, and opposite, reason. For example, the person texts or calls a close friend who doesn't respond all day. Their trigger reaction is to assume the person is avoiding them, or doesn't want to speak to them, when the person may just be busy. This is a common trigger and doesn't take much for them to reach this point.

- **Emotionally detaching.** This is seen as being cold, distant, and avoiding all methods of communication. Most times, they do this to avoid saying something they'll regret, but others it's simply a defense mechanism.

- **'Ghosting.'** We all have done this at some point, but a person with BPD does it from a different mindset and with a different purpose. This is their way of pushing someone away that's either a trigger for them, or a person they don't want to hurt if/when things get too much for them. It's another way to put their walls securely up.

- **Becoming highly irritable.** They have little patience, are quick to anger, and very thin-skinned. Those trying the hardest to support them will be the most likely to be on the receiver's end of this behavior. It could get to the point that even just checking in on them will be enough for them to scream at us to leave them alone.

- **Explosive anger.** This is a terrifying behavior to the brunt of, but they are more likely to take things out on inanimate objects or themselves than other people. It doesn't even take much to set them off, but it can be seen as yelling, purposely breaking things, throwing things, ripping things apart, hitting objects, or resorting to self-harm. This is one of the top behaviors to watch as closely as possible because they don't have enough self-control to stop themselves from causing damage, or seriously injuring themselves.

- **Canceling plans.** Quite often, this reaction happens in situations, or with people, where they feel they have to pretend to be okay. Whether it's at a family gathering or a friend's birthday party, it can be too exhausting to put a happy mask on, and keep it on, when they don't feel it. Canceling set plans is easier than having to force themselves to be someone they believe they have to be.

- **Isolating.** For many of us supporters, this can be a disconcerting response because we fear what they'll do when we let them be. In one way, it can be seen as a good thing because they know they're hurting and don't want to hurt anyone. Being alone is easier than taking things out on others. On the other hand, leaving a person with BPD alone with their thoughts gives them license to deal with stuff in harmful ways. If they ever want to isolate, let them. But we should check on them often, so they know we're just a shout away.

Some of these tactics may be all too familiar, but these are the most common signs that the sufferer is splitting. Know that these are a few steps before they take action on those displayed feelings. These are the times we try working them through those tough emotions in healthier ways. Sometimes they may want us to be right there, but not say anything. Other times they may want us to remove ourselves and let them sleep. Either way, we always need to let them know we're there whenever they need us.

In the next chapter, we'll be focusing entirely on the glories and tribulations of loving a person with BPD. Even though we constantly feel we're being tested, pushed away, or an emotional punching bag, we love them with all of our heart. And beneath it all, they love and appreciate us, too.

CHAPTER 4

Loving Someone with BPD

Too often we underestimate the power of a touch, a smile, a kind word, a listening ear, an honest compliment, or the smallest act of caring, all of which have the potential to turn a life around.

–Leo Buscaglia

As we go through the diagnosis and treatment plan processes with our loved one, it can be truly heartbreaking watching them be seen as a "BPD patient" rather than an individual learning how to cope with that one part of who they are. Somewhere along the journey, the members on the mental health team are all about medication, symptoms, and therapy and overlook who's underneath all of that: a whole person.

No matter if it's a best friend, a child, a parent, a sibling, or any other family member or acquaintance, it's a helpless feeling when you don't know how to most effectively help a person who doesn't even seem like they want you to be near them a majority of the time. But with a team that is behind us, and our loved one following a new path, we shouldn't feel powerless anymore. They are fighting something they can't see, but feel with overwhelming intensity, every single day. Following their lead, we should continue with our unconditional support. There are a few things we're going to discuss in this chapter.

First, we're going to cover a few things about helping a loved one with BPD. This isn't just about understanding their condition, or knowing how to respond effectively to behaviors, it also means hearing what they try telling us about what's going on inside of them. We also need to know how to handle the scenario when a person with BPD avoids, or outwardly refuses professional help. There's much more involved than simply telling them it's best for them, plus we don't really know what fears they may have about accepting help. We'll offer some suggestions to gently nudge them to keep going.

Finally, we're going to cover two other points. The first is that it may be helpful, both for supporters and sufferers alike, to look at some of the good traits those with BPD have. It may be a surprise for the sufferer especially that there are actually positive things hidden away among the symptoms. The second point is one many supporters are reminded of, but rarely follow suit. We're going to review the importance of practicing good self-care. How can we expect to be there for our loved one when we are already running on empty? You'll have a few suggestions on taking precious time for yourself and how it helps everyone else.

Think of this chapter as the stepping-stone for advocating for a loved one when they're strong enough to get back to living their lives as an effective part of their community. That's the end goal for every person on the mental health team.

Supporting a Loved One Through Stormy Times

We know that communication is one of the main components of any relationship. Those of us supporting a person with BPD, however, know that this is challenging on the best days. It isn't just because they don't understand what's going on inside of themselves enough to talk to us about it, there's also the feeling that anything we say can be taken completely out of context and inadvertently trigger negative thoughts.

Conversations with sufferers can be compared with having a heated discussion with a child. Sufferers often have trouble understanding nonverbal cues, and very often misread them. Our body language, the tone of our voice, even certain facial expressions can be taken the wrong way, causing them to respond aggressively and defensively. The disorder distorts the way they interpret messages, as well as what they want to say. It raises their frustration to a point where they shut down completely, and that's what we want to prevent.

They need to be truly listened to and have their feelings acknowledged, even if we don't always understand them. When we offer them that respect, and we learn how to alter how we communicate and respond to them, it does help to diminish the angry responses or meltdowns. It also helps to pick up on the best time to begin any sort of interaction with the sufferer. If they're already in an escalated state, it's not the best time to attempt a heart-to-heart chat. When things calm down, here are a few tips in practicing effective communication:

- **Listen actively and with genuine sympathy.** Active listening means giving the person 100% attention, with no distractions. No TV, no cell phones, and no devices. Those with BPD need to know they're being heard, which means to allow them to share whatever they need to with no judgment, opinions, or criticism.

- **Focus should be on feelings, not the words.** We know that individuals with BPD are telling us more than what their words say. Encourage them to just say whatever is on their mind with no worry about how it may sound coming out. Of course there are some lines not to cross over, such as being crude or inappropriate, but they should feel free to speak openly.

- **Stay calm, even if they're lashing out.** It can be difficult not to defend ourselves when they criticize or throw accusations our way, but it's important not to lose it. Losing our cool will only escalate the situation and that won't help either side.

- **If emotions rise, try using distraction tactics.** The best distraction strategies also calm and comfort. Some suggestions could be going for a walk, doing a short work out, having tea, love up the family pet, or do some cooking/baking. Distract using things they either like to do, or are good at.

- **Talk about things outside of their condition.** They get enough about their BPD through therapy, and may begin to define themselves through their condition. Even talking about 'fluff' stuff is a great way to keep communication open.

With the communication up and running, it's important that boundaries are also set. This isn't about helping the sufferer learn to create their own boundaries, it's equally as important for supporters to establish and strengthen theirs. When all boundaries are known and respected, it helps to develop trust among everyone which is the base of all healthy relationships. This is a valuable thing for those with BPD to work on.

Setting, maintaining, and strengthening boundaries is something the sufferer may not be happy with initially. This stems from their intense fear of abandonment and rejection, but we have to persevere because when we cave to their reaction we're basically rewarding poor behavior. But if we remain strong, it empowers all involved and leads to a better, trusting, respectful relationship.

A few 'do's and 'don'ts' to bear in mind include:

- **Do:**
    - assure the person that the boundaries are being set for the good of the relationship for *both* of you. Remind them that these things are what will make the relationship run more smoothly when we know what works and what doesn't on both sides.
    - have everyone on the same page with the same boundaries. It's also important to have understood consequences when they aren't respected.
    - introduce boundaries as the opportunity represents itself, rather than giving the whole list of boundaries in one shot. They'll be easier to digest, taken more positively, and receive less static.

- **Don't:**
  - make ultimatums right off the bat. Those never go off well. Boundaries will be tested to ensure that consequences will kick in when they're crossed. It's human nature. If the behavior continues even with the looming consequences that fall into place when they aren't respected, giving an ultimatum can be used as a last resort.
  - ever allow abusive behavior. State clearly that you wouldn't do that to them, so you will not tolerate it toward you.
  - enable them. There is a strong difference between *helping* a person, and *enabling* them. When we're trying to help, it means the person needs a bit of assistance to get them past a hump but will be okay with the right tools if that happens again. On the other hand, to enable a person means we take away the accountability away from the person and take it on ourselves. This doesn't help the person learn to stand on their own two feet.

Once communication tactics and boundaries are in place, there are a few other ways we can help the sufferer while protecting ourselves at the same time. These suggestions are extras to keep close on days when we aren't feeling we're getting anywhere no matter what strategies we've tried on our own, or have been guided to through the mental health team:

- When set boundaries aren't being respected, resorting to gentle verbal guidance may be required. It could even be something worded as, "You need to speak calmly and respectfully to me if you want to continue with this conversation. If you aren't able to right now, we'll have to try again later once you're less angry."
- Bring the support team together on how to set boundaries that are in unison. In this way, the sufferer will soon realize that they can't single out one person they believe will take their abusive behavior and agree as a group how to handle

situations when they arise.

- Supporters absolutely need a self-care plan, including time to themselves every day. It takes a great deal of patience, energy, and brain power to be by a sufferer's side. We need to take that time to recharge. There will be more on this point later on in the chapter.

- Most importantly, hurtful treatment is harmful to both the sufferer and to us down the road. So don't allow it under any circumstances.

Self-Care When Supporting a Loved One with BPD

As supporters of a loved one with BPD, it's natural for us to make that person our number one priority. It's an admirable job without a doubt, but it's also draining, exhausting, and takes away from our overall health. By no means is this the sufferer's fault. We need to remind ourselves the importance of caring for us, so we have the energy to care for them. And that's what self-care is all about.

Many of us feel guilty even thinking about taking time away from the sufferer. But if we can come back refreshed, full of energy, and have a positive mindset, it's good for them, too. Here are vital ways to make sure we're on top of caring for ourselves when supporting our loved one:

- **Join BPD support groups.** This may not seem like self-care, but it is. By reaching out to others who truly understand the ins and outs of what it's like to help and support a person with BPD is good for the heart and soul. There is nothing less lonely than thinking you're the only one out there in the same boat. Reach out and you'd be surprised who reaches back.

- **Be around other people.** 'Self-care' doesn't necessarily mean alone time (although, that's important too). When your entire day, and most of the night, focuses on caring for another person, we need to avoid the lure of isolating ourselves. Of course, there are tons of creative things to do that don't require being around others, but socializing is healthy. Check in with friends, family or others who have nothing to do with illness, therapy, or treatments. Step away from it all for just a little while.

- **Manage stress.** When another person's anxiety, worries, and stress are at the forefront, our own stressors are often pushed on the backburner. But as we remind our sufferer, not facing things can build up to the point our overall health is impaired. Deal with stress effectively, and if it can't be, be sure to seek professional insight.

- **You're allowed to have fun!** As an extension of the first point, we often feel guilty about going out and simply enjoying ourselves. Or maybe we've forgotten how. We're allowed to go out to a movie, go window shopping, have lunch with someone we haven't seen in a while, or just go to the park for a nature walk.

- **Pay attention to physical health.** It's easy to ignore an ache, pain, or some other physical symptom that our health is being ignored. We need to make sure we're eating properly, keeping substance consumption to a minimum, getting enough sleep, and doing an activity to get the body moving. We also need to pay attention to things that may be out of whack. We all know that little aches and pains can turn into something more worrisome when we're not paying close enough attention.

Self-care is vital to everyone on the BPD support team. We need to make sure that our mind, body, and spirit are in sync, and securely connected. The best way to remember it is by remembering the "Three C's": I didn't *cause* it. I can't *cure* it. I can't *control* it. That's an empowering expression that we could write down, and pin up where our sufferer can say it too.

Yes, There Are Positive Traits of BPD

It may surprise many supporters to see the positives in our loved one living with BPD. When we focus on all of the symptoms and negatives of the disorder, we tend to forget that this is a *whole* person, and that BPD is only a part of their whole self. And it doesn't help when society still puts tremendous stigma on mental health struggles.

Many people who have BPD are highly intellectual, intelligent, and highly empathetic individuals. This section isn't to 'glorify' mental health issues or diminish its seriousness. We just want others to view sufferers beyond their diagnosis, so they don't become defined by it.

The following are positive traits of BPD, and we should remind sufferers of every single day:

1. **Deep empathy.** As touched on above, individuals are so emotionally connected with others that they've been known to take their emotions, pain, stress, or other feelings as their own. Perhaps others feel drawn to them because they believe the sufferer will understand them at a level no one else will.

2. **Extremely resilient.** They probably can't even see this in themselves, but resilience is the trait of literally being knocked down, and having the strength and courage to get back up. Even though they see things in a black-and-white mindset, seeing self-harm as a release and suicide as a resolution, most times they stick it out and keep trying. That's powerful.

3. **Highly perceptive.** Even though in the throes of emotional meltdown, they often misinterpret what others say or do, they are more perceptive than we think. They're always watching, reading, and picking up on our vibes, and others may feel overwhelmed by the sufferer's ability to pick up on things the rest of us often miss.

4. **They see beauty in ways others don't.** Don't be mistaken. They may see

themselves as unworthy or even unlovable in their lowest times, but have an uncanny way of seeing the beauty around them in ways few others can.

5. **They understand invisible trauma.** As is the case with many mental health or psychological conditions, BPD is invisible. Others can't see the suffering, pain, or injury that's been inflicted upon them, or how deeply it's affected them. This knowledge and insight also plays a part in their compassion. They'd be superior in positions of advocacy where they are a voice for those who don't have one.

6. **Deep capacity for love.** As we've learned in earlier discussions, BPD sufferers may not have positive personal images, or falsely believe they're unworthy of love, but they love deeply. Their fears often stand in the way of expressing their capacity for love, but those who are able to get past those barriers will feel a pure form of love that may be overwhelming at first. Their love and loyalty extends to friends, family, and partners in life that they've allowed to get close.

7. **They express their pain artistically.** This is an amazing talent. Even when they don't have the words to express their deep level of pain, they can *show* it through music, art, poetry, or other forms of writing. Not only are the arts an empowering way to turn to more effective ways of coping, but their art may touch another person who needs that understanding.

There are probably other positive traits we can list, or the sufferer can contribute themselves. They hear enough about the negatives of their condition, and all the harmful ways they think and behave. Take time to remind them of all of the pluses they have, and they're more important.

This leads us to the next chapter where we learn how the condition not only affects sufferers and what we want outsiders to understand, we'll also share the most important aspects of BPD that the sufferers want others to know. These discussions are what will lead us to be strong advocates for our loved one.

CHAPTER 5

Healing Together

Being deeply loved by someone gives you strength, while loving someone deeply gives you courage.

–Lao Tzu

This chapter's focus is on healing together as supporters and sufferers moving forward after the treatment plan has been set. There may be times where tweaks to the plan may be required as life ebbs and flows, but the base routine has been established. Now we need to find the best way to advocate for our loved one, so they learn how to advocate for themselves. This is an essential part of the whole process as the individual goes out to be a productive contributor to their community with as little stigma attached to them as possible. They deserve that, and it means eliciting greater understanding from all possible angles on BPD, and what it's truly like to live with it. After all, people only fear what they don't understand. Our goal is to change that.

We'll start with sharing facts others need to know about this condition from the mind of people who live with it every day. Remember that BPD is an invisible disorder, so the first step is helping others see it as a *part* of an individual, rather than a "BPD person." There's a difference.

From there, we want others to know about and understand what it looks like to close friends and families who are supporting a person with BPD. The reason the condition can be so difficult to pin down and diagnose is that the person becomes so good at keeping their symptoms under the radar, people outside of the sufferer's "inner circle" miss what's really going on. We'll be sharing facts every person should know about this disorder so we can all advocate most effectively.

We're then going to have an in-depth discussion focusing on how we can continue to effectively give on-going support to our loved one. Even though their mental health team may not be right there as part of the daily activities, as we are, they'll still need reminders, so their confidence remains high with functioning to the best of their abilities.

Our last discussion for this chapter will be focusing on suggestions for coping skills. These are ways to empower our loved one to take control of all they learned in therapy, and put them into play when their symptoms are triggered so they don't become escalated. These coping skills can be the stepping-stones for learning the mindfulness mindset, and living life holistically which we'll be focusing on in the final chapter.

For now, let's talk about ways to inspire our loved one to break the barriers of stigma and misunderstanding.

Open Minds, Inspire Acceptance, and Stop the Stigma

If all of us were willing to see the world through the eyes of a person struggling with mental health struggles, even just for a short while, it would change the world's view of mental health dramatically. That means not just reading up on a condition, watching a show about it, or even hearing professionals talk about it. None of those views can give an outsider a true understanding of what the conditions are *really* like because they don't live with those conditions.

Many sufferers get to a point where they want to give up, not because of the condition itself but more because those who say they want to help are only adding to the chaos. They don't want to be talked over or talked about like they aren't even there when the professionals are talking about what they think is best for the sufferer. They don't just want to be treated symptomatically, and the core of their mental break is being ignored. And they get tired of not having their true needs acknowledged or met by those who are supposed to be helping them. Isn't their opinion, and the respect for their input equally as important? It should be.

They want to feel better after coming out of a hospital or treatment setting, not worse than when they went in. That being said, these are some important points they want others to see and understand:

- **BPD is sometimes linked with other conditions.** We've touched on this point earlier, but from the sufferer's perspective it's important. The NIMH estimates that 1.4% of the population have BPD, and most of these people have comorbid disorders (*Personality Disorders*, 2022). There is no prescription to 'fix' or 'treat' BPD, but there are medications for specific symptoms relating to anxiety, depression, and mood regulation. The problem is that each person experiences the condition differently, and any prescriptions will also affect them differently. Some muffle some symptoms, but will elevate others at the same time. It can be a tiring, frustrating, and endless process trying to find the best medication regimen. Also, the symptoms from the other conditions the sufferer may have will affect their BPD too. Each person will have their own "BPD toolkit," where they'll have a plan made just for them and ways of coping with their symptoms.

- **The earlier BPD is detected, the better my chances are of learning to cope.** Youth and teens as young as 12 years old have been diagnosed with BPD, but there is great caution with stamping a young person with the label. It can be seen as a 'phase' young people all go through, so they need to be analyzed very carefully. But as with any sort of mental, psychological, or physical conditions are diagnosed, the earlier intervention can be made to set the person up for higher success.

- **A BPD diagnosis doesn't make me a bad person.** This is a mindset that sufferers often fall into. They convince themselves that because they handle things much differently than others, they're 'bad' or a burden on those trying to care for them. This is false and, in fact, having such a condition makes them insightful, compassionate, and the best possible spokesperson for others going through it.

- **Having BPD doesn't mean I'm a drama-seeker.** Those with this condition would love to be able to have a handle on their own emotions, and certainly don't revel in the attention they inadvertently get from meltdowns or breakdowns. It may seem as though they desire the attention because they often seek validation and acceptance, but they certainly don't want preferential treatment. It's often misunderstood.

- **BPD makes me feel unlovable.** Because they feel so much all at once, or absolutely nothing depending on the situation, an individual with BPD isn't able to express their true feelings in a proper way. As with any other situation in their lives, they are either intense in a relationship, or completely removed from it. This makes having a real relationship with them so difficult. This is where their belief that they're unlovable comes from, and they tend to push away to avoid either getting hurt or hurting someone they care about.

- **BPD interferes with my ability to have control over my emotions and responses.** An example to show this would be forgetting a Birthday. For most of us, this wouldn't be a huge deal. We'd send belated wishes and that'd be it. Life sometimes gets so busy these things happen. For a person with BPD, the same situation would be felt at a much deeper level. They'd feel guilty for forgetting, beat themselves up unnecessarily for not being there, and not forgive themselves. This could lead to other spurts of emotional responses, but this gives a visual. We'd consider this a four or five on the emotional scale and easily rectifiable, whereas the person with BPD would shoot this over ten. It's important for outsiders to remember that these are aspects of BPD the person is learning to keep in check and to have patience if it happens.

- **There's a link between BPD and trauma.** This isn't true in every case, but there are many BPD sufferers who have trauma in their pasts. When unresolved trauma exists, the emotional and mood dysregulation seen today has a direct connection with a situation from the past where they were felt initially. That trauma needs to be dealt with first in order to pave the way for success in treatment for BPD. Those who want to understand a person with BPD and their reactions need to bear in mind that trauma may be the stem of a portion of those reactions.

Those who aren't familiar with BPD may benefit from knowing how isolating and lonely the condition can be. With the constant fear of not knowing what out there will trigger something inside of them, they often choose not to go out at all. We can help them with those confusing feelings by building up their sense of self and the belief they are an important contributor to our world.

Self-Care Suggestions for Those Living With BPD

Self-care is a group of life skills to ensure we're taking care of ourselves as best as we can. We're going to focus on mindfulness in the next chapter but for this section, we want to cover self-care tips our loved ones should keep close when they face triggers or stressors in their environment.

- **When I feel overwhelmed:** It's suggested to remind our loved one that when we focus on a situation one thing at a time, or one emotion at a time, it doesn't seem so big. Have the person breathe through the initial moment, then break the situation down into tiny, easier to deal with bits.

- **When I feel angry, frustrated, or restless:** This greatly depends on the sensory tolerance of the individual, but some tips can be ripping up paper or a plastic bag, punching a pillow, throwing a frustration foam brick, holding ice, 10 minutes of intense exercise, or doing outside chores. The idea is to distract from the initial discomfort of the emotion and to avoid trigger responses.

- **When I feel sad or alone:** This is one that depends on the person's age, as well as their tolerance for touch or other sensory input. Some options can be wrapping up in a blanket and watching a show; writing down negative thoughts, then ripping it up; listen to music that inspires or uplifts; writing a letter of comfort, or a journal entry, to the part that is sad or depressed; or cuddling a stuffed animal or pet. The key here is not only to distract from the negative emotion, but divert attention to a healthier way of coping with them.

- **When I am having a panic attack or feel stressed:** This involves methods that give comfort, and bring the person down from explosive to calm. Some ideas could be to have a favorite drink while paying close attention to the sensory input (e.g., flavor, temperature, feel of the glass); take in deep, deliberate breaths; be aware of everything around in that moment; or indulging in a hot bath or shower. The point with these suggestions is to have the person become one with how the panic or stress makes their body feel, then turn to specific ways that ease those unpleasant feelings.

- **When I "space out":** The focus would be keeping the person there in the moment and not to separate themselves from it. Some suggestions could be chewing something pungent like ginger or hot spices; clapping hands or tapping on the thighs until they can feel the sting; or drink ice water and chew on the cubes. One thing to be wary of here is not to allow the person to hurt themselves to feel/not feel. The clapping, for example, should stop once they've "woken themselves up" and not go any further.

- **When I want to harm myself:** We may have an idea if thoughts are going on to move the person this way, but we don't always catch them before they act on their thoughts. When they show signs of moving to self-harm, some things to try could include rubbing ice on the spot they want to harm; put a piece of tape on the skin, then peel it off; practice yoga or other form of meditation; or take a cold bath or shower. Again, the idea is to interrupt the thought/act line of thinking. We shouldn't do anything that feeds into the self-harm mindset but, rather, distracts from taking action.

Because our loved one can be so impulsive, these are great tools and strategies they can turn to in those fleeting moments. But what can they do in the long run, or when there isn't someone right there during those moments to remind them ways to distract themselves? Our hope is that they'll develop their own coping tools and turn to them when they need them. Until then, we can set them up by suggesting the following they can add to what they're already doing:

- talk to a trusted person whenever feelings start rising too quickly to control
- keep a mood diary where they can release all of their good and bad feelings and they're stored somewhere safe outside of themself
- plan ahead for stressful or difficult times by ensuring coping tools are in place, and that they have an effective counteractive way to deal with negative thoughts, emotions, or stressors
- create a "self-care box" where they can store all of the little things they find comfort from such as pictures of loved ones, scented candles, crystals, favorite CDs, book, or a fidget tool
- take care of physical health by ensuring healthy eating, restful sleep, exercise, enjoying nature, and avoiding all forms of alcohol or drugs
- seek out professional resources to cope with any sort of bullying or maltreatment in the community

One of the main struggles in dealing with BPD is the discrimination our loved one endures in their community. It's the main reason they won't accept or seek help, even from those of us who try being by their side regardless of the situation. The next section touches on how to lovingly deal when this happens.

When Your Loved One Resists Help for Treating or Coping With BPD

It can be excruciating as a supporter when our loved one pushes us away, and keeps us at an arm's length, no matter how hard we try offering our help. We know we can't force them to willingly accept treatment, even if the person is a youth. The control for embracing the benefits of therapy is out of our hands, but our hearts won't give up even if they give up on themselves.

During times when they resist their therapy or treatment, or "go along with it" so we and/or their mental health team will back off, we can still offer our unconditional support. Here are a few things we can try:

- **Encourage them to give treatment a try.** If we're willing to do anything possible to help our loved one, we fully support giving it a try. It may not seem to help initially, or might even seem overwhelming, but trying is better than doing nothing, right? That's the mindset we need to inspire in our loved one. They are leery about venturing into new situations more than most others are, but we need to work them through any anxiety or jaded beliefs they may have to test the waters before deciding it doesn't work.

- **Help them to understand their treatment.** We are already aware that BPD isn't easy to treat, but it's possible. If we learn all we can about the treatment to be tried on our loved one, we should become as versed with it as we can including any lingo and the process in general. What would also be helpful is if our loved one had ways they could practice their skills they're learning in therapy on their own. It gives them some power they feel they've lost, which will inspire them to keep facing forward.

- **Remind them how much we appreciate them.** Quite often, our loved ones will work really hard to make us happy. They do this to make up for any of their negative behaviors and to assure themselves that they haven't disappointed us to the point where we'd give up. The downside to this is that if we inadvertently don't acknowledge their efforts, they may take this to heart which starts the cycle all over again. They crave honest appreciation, validation, and our love so give it to them unconditionally whenever they're making their best effort.

- **Let them know that their mixed messages won't make you leave them.** They bounce back and forth between expressing their undying devotion to us, then turn around and hate us the next minute. As upsetting as this can be, they need to know that we'll be there through the times of fun and love, as well as the down and out times. They're still the same person either way, and our love for them won't disappear.

- **Be as responsive as we can be.** If the loved one reaches out to us, we should respond as best as we can. This doesn't mean that we should condone being available on call at every moment of the day and night. Their go-to when they don't feel heard is to self-harm, but if we respond how we can when we can, it can diminish those trigger maladaptive coping tools.

- **It's not their fault.** We've said this a few times throughout previous chapters, but it's a good reminder. No matter how outrageous or extreme their reactions and behaviors are, they can't control them. They have a mental health issue with active symptoms, and that's how we should see it. They aren't doing, saying, or behaving the way they are voluntarily, and certainly aren't meaning to hurt us purposely. That's why we need to constantly remind ourselves to look at them as a whole person, and resentment or blame has no place there.

In supporting and advocating our loved one, it's vital for us to take time out for ourselves too. It can be exhausting and draining sometimes, and we need time away from the situation, so we continue feeling okay about the whole thing. We need to remember the importance of maintaining our own wellbeing, which we'll go further with in the next chapter.

CHAPTER 6

Putting it All Together–BPD the Holistic Way

You gain strength, courage, and confidence by every experience in which you really stop to look fear in the face. You must do the things which you think you cannot do.
–Eleanor Roosevelt

At this point, it should be clearer what BPD is, what it isn't, and what it's really like to care for a person with this condition. Although we've given many suggestions and tips that can be incorporated into a current treatment plan, there are some other valuable methods that can also be considered. The holistic approach to any form of health has many valuable options that our loved one may embrace and practice more freely than therapy practices recommended for them alone. The main reason for their draw to the holistic is that they are treated more as a whole person with different components that each need care, rather than simply a mentally ill person.

The initial step would be to work with our loved one on mindfulness. We've brought this up in earlier chapters, but we're going to go much deeper. For a person who spends much of their time in the past, and worrying endlessly about what will come, the best gift we as supporters can offer to our loved one is how to live in the present. That means grasping the concept of living today, being open-minded to the benefits of living a mindful life, and techniques and exercises the person can do on their own. It's essential for them to learn this mindset so they're finally able to let go of what is holding them back, being strong enough to let go of the negatives, and to put effective tools into play whenever they feel overwhelmed or drawn to old ways of coping.

Next is incorporating mental toughness with mindfulness. The two go hand-in-hand because one is living life for today, while the other are the things we put into practice to get past all of life's unpredictable, sometimes difficult, bumps. This is another important lesson for our loved ones because being mentally tough doesn't mean we forget about our past and the damage it's caused. It means that we acknowledge that it happened, and will find a way to make us better. As is the same with living with BPD, it's a part of who we are and with what's to come.

The important part of the holistic approach is solidifying the connection among the body, mind, and spirit. When one of these areas is out of sync, it tends to knock the entire system out of effective production. For those living with serious mental health issues, understanding this connection, and ways to strengthen it, will change how they see everything. It could make the difference between throwing the towel in, and persevering until everything seems brighter.

We'll end the chapter with final suggestions on how to inspire our loved one to carry on living their lives in the most productive way in spite of their BPD diagnosis. That is true powerfulness.

Being Mindful, Staying Mentally Tough, and Living Holistically

Mindfulness, for those who may not be familiar with it, is focusing our attention on the present moment, and the willingness to accept it without judgment. It's come to be seen as a key element in reducing stress and experiencing true happiness. From the viewpoint of a person supporting a loved one with BPD, this is exactly what most of us hope they achieve. But, like with any sort of life change, it takes a lot of constant and consistent work. It can prove to be invaluable if our loved one fully embraces this mindset. And once they do, being more mentally tough and holistically in sync will fall into place naturally.

The benefits of living mindfully are numerous that can bring calmness to many physical and psychological symptoms, as well as increase health, attitude, and benefits. It works by embracing a sense of acceptance about all experiences—good and bad—rather than to avoid dealing with them. The three most beneficial areas include improving:

- **Well-being.** When we're mindful, we become more fully engaged in activities and it helps us deal with adverse events, situations, or people. We are also less likely to become obsessed with what might happen or what has happened, which helps us to do things that truly matter to us and where we want to be. This increases self-esteem and confidence, and develops deeper connections with others.

- **Physical health.** Mindfulness has many health benefits including dealing with stress better, lowering heart disease, lowering blood pressure, eases chronic pain, improves sleep patterns, and helps to improve the gastrointestinal system. Basically, the idea of lowering stress, worry, and concern about things beyond our control helps to alleviate the negative physical symptoms stemming from stress.

- **Mental health.** Many psychotherapists have incorporated mindful meditation practices into their therapy plans as a positive coping tool for depression, substance abuse, eating disorders, anxiety disorders, and ocd. These are all conditions that tend to veer off the present path, and learning mindful practices can help switch our focus.

There are various ways of practicing mindfulness, and it's important to find a routine that works best. For a person living with BPD, this could be somewhat of a challenge as their needs and focuses seem to change often. Whatever technique, or combination of different ones, is chosen, the end goal should be achieving a state of alertness, focused relaxation, and acceptance of what's happening in the now. In that way, the person will be able to refocus on the present moment, no matter what other distractions are around them at the same time.

All mindful practices are some form of meditation, when we sit silently, focusing on natural breathing or on a 'mantra'. The idea is to allow thoughts to come and leave freely with no judgment or concern. There are specific areas to drift focus to as the loved one relaxes into their practice. The main ones include:

- **Body sensations.** Some examples might be itching, tingling, shivers, or similar input. The idea is to allow them to come in, acknowledge them and how they affect the body, then let them pass. It's powerful to achieve because as we supporters know, it can be a tiny body sensation that doesn't feel right that can throw the bpd person into a whirlwind of negative reactions.

- **Sensory input.** It isn't possible to tune out all sensory input because our world is filled with it. Remind the person to make mental note of all things that tap into our senses, name them as they're experienced, then release them.

- **Emotions.** Our loved one with bpd is bombarded with emotions they often don't know how to process. In their meditative state, they should allow emotions and emotional responses to enter their space, name them as they come to the surface, then breathe through them as they let the emotions pass.

- **Cravings or urges.** There are so many examples in this area but for the sake of working with a person with bpd, the focus should be on cravings, behavior, and addictions. If any of these present themselves, guide the loved one to let them in so they can pay close attention to the way those things make their body feel. Once there, work them through it by wishing it away by replacing it with healthier thoughts, then help them let it go.

All of these sound easier to instruct, than to put into play but they can be done with the right aspiration and strength. They'll need help learning the basics in order to carry through on their own, and the main part is building a strong base of the ability to concentrate. Mindful meditation grows from this base of concentration skills and the practice of acceptance. Here are ways to guide them toward concentration and acceptance practices:

- **Go with it.** Once concentration is developed, the loved one will be able to connect effectively with their inner thoughts, sensations, and emotions without judging them as 'good' or 'bad.' This is an amazing realization to get to because the person would experience more sincere, happy moments that will overshadow the bad.

- **Focus.** Making themselves aware of the sensory input around them will help guide them to enjoy the moment as it is in a particular moment. It means those moments won't be tarnished with the 'then' or the 'what-ifs,' and they'll be able to distinguish between feelings of well-being and those that trigger anguish.

- **Perseverance.** Initially, our loved one may struggle with sitting still, taking in all sensations around them, and how their body responds to those things. If they stay with it, though, their perimeter of tolerance will expand a little bit each time. And if for any reason they miss or feel they aren't able to do a session, they should be encouraged to go back to it when they feel more receptive.

- **Ability to redirect with empathy.** After a while, our loved one will be able to sense when their mind is wandering off or shutting down, and they'll have the inner energy to guide them back to the moment.

Mindfulness meditation should be practiced at least 20 minutes at first, working the way up to 45 minutes. The goal is to work toward doing a session at a comfortable time six days a week. This is something that will need to be worked into since most people with BPD aren't able to focus on one thing, sit still for too long, or enjoy any of the bodily sensations. All we can do is encourage and guide them, or even do it right by their side, initially.

Becoming, and Staying, Mentally Tough

As we've learned, physical and mental health isn't innate. We have to work at it in order to develop it most effectively. Here are a few effective ways to guide our loved one to become mentally tough:

- **Practicing present-thinking.** We discussed this in the last section, but in terms of being mentally tough, the focus in this mindset is not shying away from difficult times or challenges, but to embrace them and all we're supposed to gain from them presently.

- **Our mind needs daily exercise, too.** Muscles need to strengthen and grow in order to be able to handle the next challenge. The same holds true for the mind. The strength of the mind is built through the small wins throughout the day, and to be confident with our choices. Our loved one will find it empowering to do tasks that stretch our mental capacity.

- **Embrace challenges.** The entire idea behind challenging themselves is to empower our BPD loved one with not just setting goals that are simple to reach. The idea is to challenge themselves with goals that they *might* achieve, but require the greatest effort. This grows from believing in ourselves and our abilities, which strengthens as each goal is met.

- **React positively.** This is a major component of mental toughness, and a trait that those with BPD need to learn. It can be humbling and difficult to realize that we may not have control over what happens around us sometimes, but we do have control over our responses. Our loved ones are slowly learning that they can't control others, and they'll be accomplishing amazing things once they're in tune with their reactions.

- **We are stronger than fear.** Our loved ones may not completely believe this most days but when they're resilient enough to face their fear, it will dissipate and so will its effect on them.

- **Remove 'can't' from our vocabulary.** The idea of mental toughness is to remove negative words we tend to believe over the positive ones that get us further on our life's journey. Anything is possible with the right attitude.

- **Perseverance means empowerment.** The idea of perseverance is not allowing hurdles to stop us from getting to where we want to be. Our loved one drowns in negative words that keep them down. Facing, and conquering, fear or bad moments without throwing the gloves down is inspiring.

- **Seek answers.** To get a handle on the voices they hear, which control their responses most of the time, is the bravest way to respond to stressors better.

- **Gratefulness.** There will always be a person who can do what we're doing a little bit better than we're able to. That's okay, but it's a difficult thing to accept for those living with BPD. There's no room for jealousy or anger. Our loved one needs to learn that even though there are people who do what they're able to do, the fear and self-doubt try seeping in the cracks. If we're grateful for who we are and what we're good at, we'll be happy and grateful for others too.

- **Prepare for the bad times.** Life isn't an easy ride so there will always be adversity and tough times to face. But if our loved one learns to prepare for these times, and knows how they can respond to them, they'll have an easier time.

- **Giving ourselves credit.** When moments of self-doubt arise, the best way to combat them is to remind our loved one all they've accomplished. One tough time won't eliminate those successful times, and those are what our loved one needs to hold onto.

- **Practice every day.** Reaching and maintaining mental toughness is a continuous, day-to-day effort. It's not going to just happen, and it won't stick if we leave it on the sidelines. Being in tune with ourselves, our reactions, and our goals will keep mental toughness strong.

All effort put into being more mentally tough is rewarded in countless ways, so we should make sure we're tapping into it constantly.

A Holistic Approach to Mental Health

The holistic approach is caring for ourselves as a whole person, rather than a cluster of symptoms. The idea is that when we aren't feeling right, this is usually because somewhere within the mind, body, and spirit connection there's an unbalance that seeps into the other areas. In other words, we're out of balance.

When we see the self as a whole, and treat it accordingly, we'll guide ourselves back into a balanced state and we'll feel better. This is particularly important for our loved ones with BPD who are vulnerable to not only falling out of sync, but in feeding off the negatives they feel rather than turning to their more positive coping methods. These are a few tips we can work with our loved one to achieve inner balance:

- **Value ourselves.** Remind them to turn off the tapes playing self-criticizing words, and focus more on kindness and respect for themself. Guide them to practicing their hobbies, making time for their favorite projects, and help them broaden their horizons through new experiences.

- **Value our body.** This point has been touched on earlier but doing all that's possible to maintain physical health as when it's ignored, it impacts mental health too. This includes eating healthy meals, drinking water, avoiding smoking/vaping, getting the body moving, and making sure they get enough rest.

- **Surround ourselves with good people.** It's important to have strong family and close friend connections. Knowing we're surrounded by those who accept us just the way we are, no matter what happens, makes us stronger in every way. Think of how important we are to our loved one. Don't we make them stronger to stay on track?

- **Give back.** Those with BPD are highly empathetic, and tend to gravitate to those who need a bit of extra help. Volunteering time serves a double purpose in that it gives them a way to meet new people (something they often avoid), and it just feels good.

- **Deal with stress effectively.** We've discussed this in great detail, but it's a strong element in the holistic approach. Stress is a part of life whether we like it or not. But if we guide our loved one to the best ways to cope with it, it won't be allowed to grow to the point of no return. With all the tactics we've touched on, there's one that's really effective: laughter. When we laugh we release 'feel good' hormones, we release built up stress, and it's fun. It's also contagious, in a good way.

- **Quiet the mind.** This is one of the toughest things for someone with BPD to do, but we've learned several ways to help them do this. Remind them to practice deep breathing, meditation, writing in a journal, or other ways they find will calm the mind. They need to drain their brain of excess noise.

- **Setting doable goals.** Goals need to be reachable, and have meaning to overall happiness. If goals are too easy, they may get bored and feel unchallenged. If they're too difficult, they'll be too frustrated to keep trying. Set goals that challenge, but keep them moving forward.

- **Insert little surprises in everyday routine.** Our loved ones need routine, but they can become mundane, boring, and uninspiring. Throwing a few tidbits of new help can breathe life into a routine and help to rejuvenate the person.

- **Say 'no' to drugs, alcohol, and other substances.** To put it simply, a person who already lives with a condition that wreaks havoc on their brain chemistry and their behavior, consuming substances that do the same thing but worse will only lead to disaster. If it's not prescribed by a healthcare provider, it shouldn't be put in their body.

- **Ask for help.** Whether it's reaching out to us, to a member of their mental health team, or another trusted person when they feel they're in the middle of a whirlwind, they should know when to ask for help. It's never a sign of weakness, but strength and courage.

Our loved ones are doing their very best to live in our world with skills we take for granted and they work so hard to practice. When they have the right tools, they are capable of doing everything they set their sights on, and to be an effective contributor to our community.

Chapter Summary

In our various discussions on BPD, the main goal was not just to elicit understanding about the condition itself, but more to embrace supporters trying to care for these individuals. Even the most serious and daunting ailments can be made easier to absorb when we understand them. Here's what was covered chapter-by-chapter.

Chapter One: If you're searching for help with how to support a person with BPD, you already have knowledge of the condition. This chapter goes into details about what it is, what it isn't, and how to see it even when the person tries their hardest to hide it. We go over the four different types of BPD, including the main signs of each and how they're similar and different. Finally, we share how BPD feels from the perspective of those who live with it.

Chapter Two: This chapter goes into detail about the diagnostic process. Even though supporters share the same space as the sufferer, getting the right diagnosis can be a long, frustrating road. We talk about the different players on the mental health team, what they look for, and how they come to their diagnosis. There are often other comorbid conditions that make the whole process more difficult, and those are touched on too. We give supporters suggestions on things *not* to do with a loved one who has BPD, because we have to try not to feed into their manipulative nature. Finally, we compare and contrast the condition BPD is most often misdiagnosed as (and vice versa)—bipolar disorder.

Chapter Three: Once a diagnosis has been established, the next step is putting together the most effective treatment plan for the individual. There is no cure for BPD, but it *can* be treated effectively through a combination of medicinal and therapeutic methods. We go over the most common treatments. The chapter ends on a behavior called *splitting* that we supporters know is a sign that our loved one is moving into the beginning of an episode. Knowing what to watch for, what the person is really trying to say, and how to respond are so important in supporting, helping, and advocating for them.

Chapter Four: Now that we have a diagnosis and a solid treatment/therapy plan in place, now we can re-learn how to love the sufferer with and aside from their condition. After all, they're not BPD, they're a person learning to live with it. We'll give supporters strategies and suggestions to maintain our love and support through those stormy times. The supporters need support themselves, so we talk about some self-care for them. Finally, we may not realize it but there are actually positives about BPD, which remind us of the other parts of the individual that remain constant and good.

Chapter Five: When supporting a person with BPD, there's a lot of healing that will be in play. It's not just the person being treated for BPD that needs to heal, we as their allies and greatest supporters also need to heal. The entire support team needs to heal and let go of things as we move forward. Another area discussed is eliciting the importance of self-care in the sufferer, and giving them the tools they'll need to break the stigma many still have over those living with mental health issues. Through us, they'll learn how to advocate for themselves. Finally, we talk about strategies to put into play when the person resists or tries stopping treatment.

Chapter Six: The most important aspect of treatment/therapy for any condition is learning and maintaining the holistic approach. This involves the balance of the mind, body, and spirit connection, and seeing the person as a whole being made up of various elements. The focus in this chapter is offering suggestions with teaching the individual how to live life mindfully, embracing a mentally tough mindset, and maintain the whole self by living holistically.

Conclusion

Moving Forward Fearlessly

You are the one thing in this world, above all other things, that you must never give up on. When I was in middle school, I was struggling with severe anxiety and depression and the help and support I received from my family and a therapist saved my life. Asking for help is the first step. You are more precious to this world than you'll ever know.

–Lili Reinhart

The journey we've taken you on throughout our discussions may have been difficult. It's not to say that it wasn't familiar, because as the supporter of a person with BPD, we are all experts on our experience with this condition. We may not have the inside scoop, so to speak, that our loved one does but simply by being right by their side, we've seen how they suffer.

We've talked them down when that condition has taken them to a realm of distraught that consumes them. We take care of them when they're so far down, we're terrified to leave them alone. We've used our inner strength to breathe some purpose into their deflated self-worth, and offered our own life force to give them courage they don't have. We've taken the tools of self-harm away so they don't hurt themselves; we've chased them down the street when they can't take it anymore; we sleep on the floor by their bed or outside their door, so they won't escape our ever-watching eye; and we stay by their side when they try ending their pain. *That* is BPD. But it doesn't tell outsiders what it's really like, or how it really feels.

One of the most prominent reasons those with mental health conditions as serious as BPD don't seek the help they need is because of the stigma society still puts on mental illness. Sadly, it's what many people do when there is a lack of digestible information they can draw from to make a more educated perspective. And even when they're willing to take in that information, they still need to be open-minded enough to embrace and accept the person as *someone living with mental health struggles*. Just because an individual has a specific diagnosis, they should never be defined by it. Yet we still struggle with that line of thinking even in these modern times.

Through our discussions, suggestions, and tips presented in these chapters, we hope we've given supporters the voice they may not always have had to advocate for their loved one. Every effort we've made to keep our loved one facing forwards, whether they say they wanted us there or not, is rewarded hundreds of times when they pick themselves up and reach for our hand.

A person who has been supported, loved, and treated as a whole person will develop the courage to advocate for themselves. It *will* happen. Maybe not today, or even tomorrow, but it will.

Our Gratitude for Our Loved One's BPD Diagnosis

In Chapter Four, we touched on a few of the positive traits those with BPD have, and that we should celebrate in them. An amazing extension on this point is that these incredible people have a certain level of gratitude for their BPD diagnosis. That may sound somewhat contradictory after learning all the ins and outs of this condition. But when we get to the point where we can actually see the positives buried within the darkness of a very difficult mental health condition, it means the baton of power has changed. The person goes from "being controlled" by that invisible force to "being in control" of themselves, and that's powerful.

Gratitude is learned from coping with BPD, which may not always be practiced but it helps the person get through the tough days, appreciate tiny things in the good ones, and anything in between. Acknowledging even small things we have to be grateful for is a sign of hope that they need to hold on to. With hope, they can accomplish anything that falls in their path, then gratitude for getting through it as unscathed as possible.

That all being said, we'd like to leave off with a few specific points to remind our loved ones of what they should be proud of themselves for, ironically stemming directly from their BPD. Those are having gratitude for:

- **those they've met along their journey with BPD.** It's not just us who are by their sides whenever we're needed. They'll have an army of peers from their therapy sessions, the practitioners, the therapists, nurses, doctors, counselors, helpers on the therapy team, and the list goes on. They may have never met any of these people in any other avenue of life if they didn't share the core focus of BPD. This elite group of people truly understand what this condition is, and what it takes to survive the fights and the all-out battles. It's a gift to walk a line with other people who are doing the best they can, and making it work.

- **a sense of spirituality.** This is something learned during the holistic approach, and the alternative forms of treatment used. Spirituality doesn't necessarily mean religion. It's a connection with a force that is outside of ourselves, and bigger than we are. That connection brings us a sense of inner peace, balance, and connection to the world that we often feel disconnected from. BPD, then, can be seen as a source for this part of our whole self.

- **the other creative gifts that bring us completion and purpose.** Even if the individual has written, painted, played an instrument, sang, or whichever creative path they're on prior to their diagnosis, it intensifies. The person is taught to turn to and draw from these gifts to work through their difficult emotions, thoughts, and behavior and stop the immediate move from thought to response. For example, the person will become consumed with self-hate and not see the point in continuing life. Rather than taking permanent action, they open their journal and write through the thoughts and the feelings attached to them. Once the pen is laid down and the book closed, those thoughts may not be as prominent anymore. Creative gifts can literally save our loved one, and give them a sense of purpose and light.

There are so many examples of gratitude, which look different from each person living with BPD. What one person is grateful for isn't the same as for another. There may even be those who aren't at the point to see any gratitude or positivity in their condition. This could be something else to guide them to work on as it's a beautiful source of inspiration, empowerment, and strength to look back on.

BOOK #2

Setting Boundaries

How to Set Boundaries With Friends, Family, and in Relationships, Be More Assertive, and Start Saying No Without Feeling Guilty

Introduction

Understanding and using personal boundaries is a lot harder than one would think. Today, many people are aware of the concept of personal boundaries, including the need to enforce them constantly within all types of relationships. But the heart of boundaries, and one of the reasons why it is so important to have and maintain them is often forgotten: Your boundaries are actually a form of self-care.

It might sound funny, but it is true. Self-care includes your subconscious and your inner emotions. Boundaries are essentially the understanding of what you are willing to be responsible for, or not (Cloud & John Sims Townsend, 2002). Note that the actual definition will be more fully stated in the next chapter, but for now, let's get this foundation of knowledge started. You have almost the perfect formula for a form of self-care, which will protect your interests while helping you maintain healthy relationships and a holistic life-balance.

Some of you may be wondering why the beginning of this book is highlighting the connection between boundaries and self-care. Because this is arguably one of the most important forms of self-care to be practiced daily, yet it is most often the one that is constantly ignored.

But... Why are boundaries and their care ignored?

Primarily, because of the bad reputation boundaries have gotten. People are often hesitant to enact their own boundaries because they are afraid of the freedoms they will be taking away from other people, or, they have been led to feel guilty over standing up for their boundaries.

A great way to combat these feelings is by labeling your boundaries as a form of self-care. The minute you begin to reframe your boundaries as something you need to maintain for your own good—and something to ensure that you are at your best to be present in your overall life—it is much easier to stand up for them and ensure that they are maintained in the long term.

Additionally, giving them this label will help begin to remove one of the biggest 'problems' with setting and enforcing boundaries: That we often feel guilty for doing so.

While this will be covered in later chapters, this is something that needs to be addressed right here and now: Setting a boundary is nothing to feel guilty about. It is normal, natural, and a sign that you are creating a healthy relationship. Yes, knowing these things will not make the guilt go away instantly. In fact, it is something that you are going to have to actively fight for a long time while figuring out your boundary journey. However, it does get easier. Eventually, setting and enforcing your boundaries will cause a lot less guilt and will actually—believe it or not—create relief.

So trust in the process, and trust that you are doing the right thing for yourself. Because you are.

A Few Mentions

How to Use the Book

Before going any further, it is important to note the actual structure of how this book is written, and how it will apply to you.

In this book, we will discuss boundaries, boundary myths, how to be more assertive, and how to set and enforce your own boundaries. There will be scenarios and examples which will be used to specifically show where things went wrong, or how certain things could work. While reading these examples, keep your journal close so that you can write down what similarities you have, what you think will work, and what you need to think on. These scenarios will try to cover as many concepts as possible, but since boundaries are an incredibly personal and individual concept, it will be important for you to really think and analyze your own situation before going ahead and enacting any of the recommendations.

Journaling

As mentioned above, having a journal can be considered a companion to this book. When it comes to figuring out your personal boundaries, why some of your boundaries may not be met, and how you are going to enforce them in your own life, journaling is going to be a key component of helping to keep your thoughts straight. You can use a hand-written journal, or something like your phone, tablet, computer, or even an audio recording device, to keep your thoughts and concepts safe.

For this journey, writing down your thoughts will be a key element in helping you isolate the qualities of the boundaries you have—because we all have them—and begin to expand and more strongly identify the specifics of those boundaries. It is only once we actually sit down and begin to analyze certain scenarios and emotions, that we are able to isolate and give phrases to the boundaries we need to express the most.

Additionally, journaling through the examples and how they correlate to your own situations will help you begin to discern what methods and considerations will work best for you and your situation.

Terms

In this book there will be several terms used, which may be self-explanatory; but just in case, they will be described here and can be referred to as you go.

Safe People

The term "safe people" has been around for years, but the problem is that so often—like boundaries—it is not well defined. So, that will be done now. Safe people are people who we can connect with on a deeper level, who are able to tell us the truth in a way where we hear and understand them, and who allow us to be human, while also expecting and helping us become a better person (Cloud & John Sims Townsend, 2022/1995). In other words, safe people are the ones that you feel you can tell anything to. They are the sounding board of wisdom and are the ultimate veto-power of knowledge which you trust. These people also call you to a higher standard of yourself. Sure, they will laugh and joke with you, but at the end of the day, if you are doing something questionable, they will call you out on it.

Safe people are also those with whom we have a deep connection. It is not really recommended to make a safe person out of someone you just met. Would you take the advice of someone you just met in spin class on a very personal or sensitive subject? That is not to say that those types of relationships may not become safe people over time, but that should not be the immediate case.

Safe People and Boundaries

So, why do you need safe people? Well, when you look at the definition of what they do for our lives, they are honestly indispensable regardless of where you are on your mental health, or boundaries, journey. However, when it comes to enacting, enforcing, and even thinking about what your boundaries are, a safe person is a great sounding board to bounce ideas off of. Since they know you pretty well, and are already someone who can call you out on those interesting scenarios, they may have a good inclination of certain areas that need, or need better, boundaries.

That does not mean you need to go to them explicitly for advice. However, if you have certain areas or boundary ideas that you are unsure of, these are great people to go to.

Small Note

Yes, there will be many of these in this book, so might as well get used to them now. Therapists, psychologists, and counselors are the only people who can be safe people almost immediately. Why? Because that is what they are trained to do. As long as you have done your homework (e.g.,, made sure of what university they went to, how long they have been practicing, and looked up reviews), it is pretty much guaranteed that, outside of something that would be the next Hollywood special, these people are safe. They will guide you through this process as well. So do not be afraid to reach out to one if you think you need that level of help.

The Flags

These may be terms that are a little outdated, but generally the flags are used like the traffic light system, and can be used in personal relationship assessments as well as emotional responses to the world around you.

When it comes to boundaries, the flags can be used in two ways: First, you can use them to help assess your emotional responses to someone else's boundaries, your boundaries, your feelings in a situation, etc., like: "*I got angry when so-and-so told me I couldn't come over again tonight. How do I feel about this situation? Am I happy to leave them be, or am I pushing their established boundaries?*"

Second, the flags can be used to identify how certain people react to the performance of your boundaries, like: "*My friend was furious when I told him I needed some space. He said I didn't care about him at all, and if I did, I'd put my feelings aside for his. Which flag would I give to their reaction to my boundaries?*"

Red Flag

Similar to red lights, *red flags* are things you have noticed in a relationship that are a problem. But this is not just something you note and move on from, these are the "stop immediately and leave," types of problems. For instance, if there is abuse, duplicity, or deceit. In relation to boundaries, a red flag is equal to an unsafe person, or someone who does not respect your boundaries. These people may be well-meaning, but they will never be respectful and will always push. For those types of scenarios it is up to you on what to do, and honestly, on the level of boundary (which will be covered in the first chapter) that they are ignoring. If it is a big boundary (like sexual or physical consent) then find a safe person, or mediator, and end that relationship, or put very strict guidelines on it.

Red flags are the warning signs, and if you are noticing lots of red flags, get help and make sure you tell a safe person about it to stop any potential backlash. Additionally, a safe person can be a neutral third-party who can help you figure out logistics on how to get out.

Yellow Flags

In comparison to red flags, yellow flags are where things are more up to personal discretion. The reason for this is because yellow flags tend to either become red flags (big problem) or green flags (it resolves itself). Now, it is important to note that if a yellow flag becomes a red flag, listen to the advice in the above section and get out. However, for the most part, yellow flags tend to be scenarios where you can either wait and see how it goes, or avoid that situation altogether. This is mainly because yellow flags tend to be either phases of life (e.g., jobs, finances, etc.), or integral problems within yourself or others that you or the other person are willing to fix.

When it comes to boundaries, yellow flags are often when something needs to be addressed, but then is resolved through open communication and understanding.

If you are still unsure if something is a yellow flag, a great way to figure it out is by talking with the person where the yellow flag has popped up. If they are open to resolution, then the situation was a yellow flag which turned into a green flag. If they are not willing to resolve, then it is a red flag and you can consult the above section on what to do.

Green Flags

Compared to red and yellow, green flags do not really need an explanation, but a brief one will be given just in case. Green flags are the things that are great, perfect, or workable in a relationship. Ergo, they do not need work or any type of conflict resolution.

Small Note

It is normal for relationships to have a mixture of yellow and green flags, and since boundaries are a form of relationships, the same can be said for that. The big thing to notice when it comes to boundaries compared to relationships, is that yellow flags in response to boundaries—or as a boundary—should be resolved immediately, instead of waiting for them to resolve themselves.

General Note for This Book

Something that really needs to hit home before continuing, is that this book aims to help you understand and implement your own boundaries. However, boundaries are a personal responsibility as well as a personal choice, as you will see in the next chapter where the definition of boundaries are given. Therefore, there may be times in your own life during very specific instances or events, where implementing your boundaries may be tricky, and a bit more nuanced than what you may be comfortable with on your own.

If this ever happens to you, go to your safe person or to a licensed therapist and ask for clarification. Just with any type of new emotion-based habit, there will be times when your boundaries are a bit confusing, or do not make a lot of sense. That is nothing to be ashamed of, and asking for help is not a waste of money or time—as long as you go to the right person—because they will help you understand the specifics of your situation and how to handle them.

CHAPTER 1

Understanding Boundaries

As with learning anything new, understanding what you are going to learn about is the first step. Here are a few ways to begin understanding boundaries. Specifically, in this chapter, we will talk about concepts like why you *need* boundaries, and what healthy and unhealthy boundaries look like.

Why You Need Boundaries

To start us off is the question, "Why do we need boundaries?" The answer is found in the definition. According to Doctor Henry Cloud, boundaries are simply the difference between what is yours, and what is not yours (Cloud & John Sims Townsend, 2002). This applies to everything from tasks to emotions to time to finances. So then, if the answer is so simple, why is it so hard to define, live out, and even understand why they are needed?

Because real life is messy and more importantly, society often has different opinions of what is our problem versus what are other's problems. Yet, when we think of boundaries in a different way, it is pretty easy to begin defining what is yours versus what is someone else's.

Try the following exercise: Every time you consider a boundary, think of it like your personal property line. Most people are highly aware—and even make it their duty—to determine what is their responsibility versus someone else's (like a neighbor or the municipal government) when it comes to their homes. If you begin to think of boundaries in a simple black and white landscape like home ownership, figuring out what is your personal boundary versus someone else's can become a bit easier.

So What Is the Problem?

This is going to sound repetitive—so prepare yourself—but the problem with boundaries and enacting them often comes down to what people are willing to be responsible for, or not. Boundaries involve a deep amount of personal responsibility, as well as personal recognition and freedom. For instance, it would be so easy to say that your happiness is defined by someone else and their actions; and while that may have a smidge of truth—like how the actions of that person will help influence how happy you are in one particular moment. That generalization of making your happiness a byproduct of someone else's actions, and therefore their responsibility, is a poor boundary, and a good way to ensure that you are never happy.

See the problem? Unfortunately, if you are one of those people who would prefer for their innermost happiness and peace to be defined by others, you are not going to have the best of times with the rest of this book. Good news is, though, that you will be given tools and examples to help realize where you might be implicating that habit, and how to stop it.

What Boundaries Are

Which brings us to what your boundaries actually *are.* As previously mentioned, boundaries are essentially what you are willing/should be responsible for in your own life. This includes your emotions, your responsibilities, your actions, and how you are going to handle relationships.

Healthy Boundaries

Healthy boundaries are what we are striving for. So then, what is a healthy boundary? Easy. Healthy boundaries are boundaries you are willing to enforce—and do consistently—which help your overall being live up to its fullest potential. They encompass everything that you should and are willing to be responsible for in each area of your life, and they have been healthily communicated to those in close contact with you, and you have ensured that they are flexible enough to weather any scenario that comes your way.

Yes, it sounds like a lot—and to be completely honest, it is a lot of work to set up and maintain in the beginning—but it will bring infinite happiness and relief for the rest of your life, so the work and due diligence will be worth it.

In sum, healthy boundaries are the complete understanding and enforcement of your own boundaries in every scenario, no matter how big or small; and in every scenario where they are healthily communicated, your boundaries are respected and acknowledged.

Big and Small Boundaries

Which brings about something to begin thinking about now: the difference between big and small boundaries. First of all, each of these types of boundaries are important; the size of your personal boundaries should never have any effect on what you insist other people respect in their interactions with you. The sizing term allocated to these boundaries are really used as a type of emotional marker to help you better organize how you can/should respond to the violation of those boundaries.

Big Boundaries

Big boundaries are the important, non-negotiables that should never be crossed. If a larger boundary is crossed, that is a red flag, deal breaker, the neon red sign that something is wrong in the relationship or circumstance. Why is it such a big deal?

Because big boundaries are important things like consent, transparency, and respect that you have with the other individual or individuals, depending on the scenario.

Would you really be okay if someone ignored your consent? Would you really be okay if your partner cheated on you? Would you really be okay if your family lied to you and stole all your money?

Most likely the answer to all of those questions was a big fat 'no', and it should be.

These types of boundary violations are significant, mainly because these boundaries are the life-altering issues that thankfully most societies still intrinsically protect and enforce. There is a big chance that you are not even sure what all of your big boundaries are, and that is okay.

Think about whatever is a dealbreaker to you in any scenario. If you suddenly feel: unsafe, unwanted, or like there is a big problem, that scenario is first of all dangerous—so get out and get somewhere safe and contact someone safe. But also, that scenario is the destruction of a big boundary.

Small Boundaries

In comparison, a small boundary could be simply when someone is rude to you in a store. This type of boundary is something that is expected, and generally enforced by good manners or social etiquette. However, when they are crossed, you have the ability to either ignore it and be fine with that small slight, or be able to confront the person without too much backlash or drama (hopefully) in the physical setting. So, for the example of someone being rude to you in a store, you have the option of either ignoring and going about your day with only a few negative thoughts as you walk away, or the ability to confront them with something mild, such as: "I do not deserve your rudeness." Unless you do, in which case, you really need to start considering how you treat service workers.

Small Note

The dismissal of your smaller boundaries is not something to scoff at; in fact, many people are justifiably annoyed when those are ignored. However, in many societies, these are the small slights which could begin to be perceived as 'petty' or not being able to let certain things go. And that is wrong. No matter how big or small your boundaries are, they should be respected and not deliberately crossed. The problem is with how we communicate and react to those boundaries being ignored.

If you get annoyed at your small boundaries being crossed, that is not something to be ashamed of. That is a healthy response and not something you should let other people belittle you for. However, if your reactions to those boundaries being crossed are disproportionate, then you should take a moment right now and mark down in your journal why these small slights cause such a large reaction.

Often, when our reactions are larger than the actual scenario, something is building behind the scenes in our subconscious, and it is that particular build-up which is inadvertently coming out. And it is this build-up that we want to address and begin to take down.

Boundaries Can Be Fluid

Part of breaking down that subconscious and/or internal build-up of boundaries being crossed is beginning to understand that some boundaries can be fluid. Your boundaries are built from your beliefs, understandings, and background. What this means is that some of your small boundaries—and even your big ones—may change to accommodate or acknowledge your past or new knowledge. That is okay, and honestly, that is what we want for some of them.

That does not mean that you should change your boundaries for every new person or circumstance, but that also does not mean that you should maintain an old boundary if it is now harmful to you. And for some of us, it is understanding this difference which can cause a lot of disproportionate responses to our boundaries being crossed.

For example, say that you previously lent out money to friends relatively willingly, within reason. Then, over time, you began to notice that people were taking advantage of that generosity and were not respecting your own financial goals and situations. You then alter your previous boundary, but still helped out one particular friend who desperately needed the help due to recently losing their job during a volatile life situation.

In the above example, you altered your boundaries in response to a pre-existing boundary not being respected. However, at the same time, you were able to maintain an understanding and flexibility to help out the friend who really needed your help. This is what boundary fluidity means, and beginning to understand and enact that type of fluidity will most likely help you begin to lose the constant feeling of annoyance which lurks beneath the surface.

Your Personal Boundaries

Now that you know what healthy boundaries are, it is time to begin applying that knowledge to yourself. Your boundaries are based on your integral beliefs, what you are or are not willing to do, values, opinions, and perspectives (Blundell, 2019).

What this also means is that your boundaries can be influenced and change depending on life circumstances, traumas, or learning lessons you encounter along the way (Blundell, 2019). Good news is that it means that while some of your boundaries may be more permanent than others, they are not necessarily life-long commitments or decisions you have to immediately make.

If you are struggling with how to begin thinking about your boundaries, take a moment and ask yourself these three questions: "What is 'me'?" or, "What is not 'me'?" and, "What do I 'own' and take responsibility for, versus what will I not?" (McLaughlin,

2000). Seriously, take a moment with your handy journal and begin to write down the answers to those questions.

Make sure you do this, because those answers are actually the foundations of your boundaries.

What Your Boundaries Look Like

Now that you are beginning to have a vague idea of what your boundaries may be, it is time to see what your boundaries may actually look like—the phrasing to describe them and the understanding of what your boundaries are. Intrinsically, boundaries exist in every scenario we encounter and thankfully, they are often categorized as such. For instance, the boundaries you have at home versus at work probably have some differences. However, beginning to separate and differentiate boundaries becomes tricky.

First of all, differentiating and categorizing your boundaries becomes problematic because a lot of these areas overlap. For instance, many of us have physical, financial, and time based boundaries, like the work/life balance, consent on romantic dates or with family members, not lending out more than 'x' amount of money at a time, etc.). But as you can see in the parenthesis, certain things like the difference between work and life begin to mesh themselves into the abstract boundary of 'time'.

Good news is that these first scenario boundaries are all good definitions of firm boundaries. Sure, they may be subject to change depending on circumstances, but for the most part, these are pretty steadfast rules that you are willing to live by, and will consistently enforce no matter the scenario. You merely have to begin teasing them out of your subconscious mind.

When it comes to setting these more firm boundaries, take a look at areas in your life which matter the most, such as: physical, sexual, emotional, financial, and intellectual (Pattemore, 2021). These are all big concepts of your life, which transcend company like family, friends, romance, and work.

Before you get overwhelmed on how to begin defining your boundaries in each of these areas, think of it this way: You are looking for situations where you give an immediate and hearty 'no' in response to the situation. For every 'no' that you come up with, you have a boundary.

For instance, if you get upset when someone dismisses your thoughts or opinions immediately, without elaborating or discussing them with you (even if that means to help you better understand), then that is an intellectual boundary you have.

Now, this is where boundaries get tricky, because they concern the basic understanding of your responsibility versus others reactions and their own responsibility towards you; plus the ever so difficult circumstance of healthily communicating your boundaries appropriately (if this concerns you, do not worry, we will get there). A good rule of thumb when it comes to your own boundaries is that boundaries and communication go together like popcorn and butter, or peanut butter and jelly, or whatever other food combination you absolutely cannot do without. As long as you communicate your boundaries in a clear and precise way, without being rude, you are in the clear.

For instance, say that you have a pretty firm physical boundary of not hugging people unless they are immediate family. When you meet a friend of a friend, you notice that they are hugging everyone in the circle. Unconcerned, when it comes to your turn to be introduced, you smile and politely say "I do not hug other people, but I am glad to meet you." In this example, you are not being rude to the new person you are meeting, you are being firm and friendly over a personal boundary you are not willing—and honestly should not have to—compromise (Campbell, 2021).

Expressing your boundaries does not have to be painful, conflict-based, or even something to feel anxiety over (although you might the first few times, and that is perfectly okay if you are not accustomed to setting or enforcing your boundaries). It will get easier as you go along, and remember: your personal boundaries are yours alone.

Your Boundaries, Your Happiness

It may seem a little too good to be true, but there you have it. Your boundaries—and yours alone—will ensure that you are happy in the long run.

Understanding, enforcing, and even adapting them, will help you maintain a strong sense of self, as well as help you keep an inner eye on what you need or want, in any given scenario. However, this type of happiness and personal freedom does not come easily, or even immediately. It will take a lot of hard work and persistence to ensure that you maintain this happiness. Over time, this work will become easier—and perhaps even automatic in some scenarios—but be forewarned: it will require an adjustment period to get there.

It is important to remember that you are setting your boundaries for yourself. No one else. You are not setting these boundaries for your friends, your partner, your family, or even your children or dependents. Yes, they will benefit from you setting them, but they are not *for* them. They are for you.

You, Your Boundaries, and Your Emotions

Boundaries and emotions have a strong bond, particularly because we display our emotions when our boundaries are crossed.

Think about it this way: When you get annoyed at something, there is some sort of action or scenario which triggers those emotions. A majority of the time, when we feel a negative emotion but are unsure why, it is because some type of boundary or particular protocol that we as individuals inherently follow, has been crossed. But this particular protocol is not something which is universally acknowledged or understood, which then means that anytime it is disrespected we are faced with two options: to either let it pass, or to somehow deal with the emotions that are now triggered.

The problem is that as adults, we are taught to ignore or not display those emotions, especially over small slights. Which honestly, is not healthy and slightly wrong. Yes, as adults, we should probably not have a massive meltdown in the grocery store every time we do not get the cookie. Mainly because—we *are* adults, we can buy the cookie if we really, really want too. But being frustrated at the reasons as to why you probably should not buy the cookie, such as: you are trying to not eat as much sugar, you already have other cookies in your cart, you do not have the money for it this month, etc., are completely valid. Any of those reasons would be more than enough to be annoyed that you cannot buy what you want at that particular moment. However, just because you are annoyed is not an excuse to then disrupt everyone else's life and day by throwing a massive fit in the middle of the store. And for the most part, the majority of adults do know that. The social niceties and expectations have become ingrained in us over time—which is partly why the outliers who do not acknowledge or understand these niceties—are so harshly ostracized.

Which then brings us back to our boundaries and emotions. When our boundaries are crossed, negative emotions will arise, and how we respond and display those emotions are where the true work behind enforcing our own boundaries while respecting others will come into play.

Before going any further, there is something you should know: Your emotions are always valid.

Being frustrated that you cannot buy, do, or react the way you want is completely normal and arguably healthy. However, it is how you display those emotions where inappropriate behaviors and mindsets can occur. It is also in this sphere where boundaries come into play. Being upset that a boundary was disrespected is completely valid; in fact, that upset is even encouraged, because you need to understand the 'why' attached to your emotions (i.e.: your boundary being destroyed). However, if you were to disproportionately display those negative emotions, you begin to escalate a situation way beyond what it was meant to be (depending on the situation, obviously). More in-depth scenarios will be given in later chapters, but what is vital to understand here is that understanding the 'why' behind some of your emotions will help you begin to identify certain boundaries that are important to you, and are most likely the ones you should address first.

Being able to self-monitor your own emotions is a grueling task, but the rewards—especially in regards to boundaries—are endless. For instance, you will be able to better pinpoint why certain emotions are being triggered, how to calm yourself down, and also have a better understanding of how certain scenarios are toxic and/or triggering for you and how to fix or avoid them in the future. Additionally, understanding how your boundaries were crossed will give you an amazing step-up in combating how to communicate your boundaries to those around you, to ensure a healthier space for you and everyone else.

You, Your Boundaries, and Others

Which then brings up the ever so fun discussion of how your boundaries work with other people. In this section, we are going to cover a basic understanding, as in-depth relationships will be discussed in a different chapter.

In sum, you need to understand that everything we are doing here, is for your own boundaries, and that these boundaries are yours and yours alone. That is it. That is all. They. Are. Yours.

What this also means is that how people respond to them is intrinsically not your problem. If someone reacts poorly, while that is really unfortunate, that is not your fault.

Your Boundaries, Your Responsibility

Now, this is not an indication for you to say, "Yes, I know, they are mine," and leave it at that; your boundaries are your own responsibility. It is no one else's job to give you your boundaries, to uphold your boundaries, or to even necessarily know your boundaries.

Discovering, enforcing, and continuing your boundaries is your job, and yours alone. Yes, people and experiences can help you shape certain boundaries which you will continue to uphold, and you can always go to safe people, a therapist, or even a knowledgeable trusted friend (but be careful with that one), to help you define, understand, or even figure out what your boundaries are or should be. This is in no way saying that you need to find your boundaries completely on your own, or that you should not even take certain people's perspective into consideration.

What it means is that while there are hopefully a group of people to help you on this journey, figuring out and displaying your boundaries will ultimately live and die with you. Your friends can respect them, and even help remind you of them in the beginning if you need them too, but at the end of the day they will not feel the same level of upset, hurt, or frustration, when your boundaries are crossed. Their lives will go on, and their other relationships will remain relatively unaffected by your boundaries not being enacted or respected.

However, the same cannot be said for you.

On this journey of discovering your own boundaries, you need to recognize that you are personally responsible to yourself and others around you, for your end of the bargain.

Most relationships work on a relative understanding of the other's boundaries. For instance, most relationships go through the "what are we" talk where certain boundaries and expectations are discussed and set; and it is pretty clear that if any of those terms are violated, the relationship will be in danger. Apply that principle of setting boundaries clearly and succinctly in the other relationships in your life as well, and enact that level of responsibility.

Boundaries and Communication

Yes, the above statements are all true: You should act and protect your boundaries when necessary, and you should definitely be on the lookout for when your boundaries are not being met or are flat-out being ignored. However, what this also means is that you have to be aware of your own personal responsibility to yourself and others around you. People can only respect or ignore a boundary that is explicitly stated and understood by everyone in the conversation or scenario. So, if you have boundaries, but do not share them with those that you interact with on a daily basis, you cannot be completely upset when those boundaries are ignored.

Before that tangent gets out of hand: The above statement is in no way absolving when someone ignores your lack of consent, refuses to understand or attempts to understand you when you communicate boundaries to them, or when a bully truly does not care about them. What the above statement specifically points out is that in order for you to have the freedom that personal boundaries give, you have to be willing to be held accountable to the responsibility of enforcing them on a daily basis; specifically, communicating them constantly.

For instance, say that you became mad with your friend because they told something you had mentioned to them—in confidence—to mutual friends. If you had not explicitly told your friend that the nugget of information was confidential, it would not necessarily be that friend's fault for sharing the information with others (there is that ever so small argument of not talking about others when they are not present, but for the sake of this argument, we are going to ignore that particular social nicety which some people adhere to). In comparison, if you had explicitly told that friend that the information was top-secret level of confidentiality, including within the friend group, and that friend then goes around and shares the information with everyone anyway—they have clearly crossed a very specific and particular boundary. Which, in the second instance, would make any anger or frustration you feel towards that person one hundred percent valid.

See the difference? In the second scenario, you transparently laid out the boundaries that came with the information you had to share; and the friend deliberately ignored them. Whereas in the first instance, you were not explicit in the boundaries of the information, and therefore while it created a mess, the friend who spilled the beans is not entirely at fault.

This type of communication is exactly what is meant when it comes to the personal responsibility of having and communicating your own boundaries. Now, does that mean that you should go up to a store clerk and say "I expect to be treated with respect," without the clerk having done anything to warrant that comment? No, it does not. Thankfully, the majority of us live in societies where common courtesy is still expected and enforced, which makes it easier for you to withhold over-sharing your boundaries to every person you meet. More specific examples of what these 'others' could mean will be covered in later chapters, but for the introduction it was important to begin setting the stage for the responsibility you have of communicating your boundaries.

Your Boundaries and Others

On the other hand, just because you are strong in your boundaries and ensuring they are respected, does not give you the right to trample other peoples' boundaries in the process. Enacting your boundaries is going to be a fine dance of communication, understanding, and respect between yourself and those around you.

For instance, let's say that a friend called Molly and her parents have some pretty strict boundaries about phones at the table during dinner. While Molly respects that boundary she has now taken a remote job where there is a bit of a time difference, Molly is three hours ahead of the company. While the company is okay with Molly not being in the same time-zone, they do ask that she is available to be alerted for work questions or problems during their working hours. Molly agreed to those terms, and made sure that the company understood that while she would respond to a message, she might not get to it right away all the time. Again, the company understood.

So far, so good. Both Molly and the company have established great lines of communication, understanding, and work boundaries on Molly's availability and the problems of time-change in relation to work projects.

The problem comes up on the weekly Wednesday night dinners Molly and her parents had pre-arranged. Previously, Molly respected her parents' boundary of no phones at the table. However, this particular week, Molly's parents asked that the dinner be moved earlier in the day. When Molly told her parents that earlier was fine, but that she would have to be available for work, her parents agreed.

Fast forward to the dinner and Molly is in the middle of telling her parents that while her phone is on silent, it will have to sit face-up on the dinner table so that she can be alerted if there is a work notification; since that was part of the deal with working for a long-distance company. Molly's parents were not as understanding. In fact, her father insisted she turn it off until dinner was over, which would be about an hour and a half, since the family tended to have longer dinners. Molly told her father that that would not work, because the company expected a reply relatively promptly, since it was their afternoon. Molly even suggested turning her phone on vibrate and placing it on the granite countertop in the kitchen (so that she could hear the vibrations) and answer it in another room. Even to this solution, Molly's parents were displeased, and to please them, Molly ended up messaging her boss and turning her phone off.

Now, to some, that may have seemed like a healthy situation, as many people are now not as fond of having phones at the dinner table if at all possible. The problem is the inflexibility Molly's parents had to the scenario, considering it was her job and not a plethora of social texts or calls.

Molly had a boundary, which she was willing to be flexible on, to accommodate both her job and her parents. Her company was being beyond flexible in Molly's needs. The problem was that Molly's parents were completely inflexible towards the scenario. While it is all well and good to have your own boundaries (and certainly as parents, the ability and need to have more veto-power is definitely necessary up until a certain age), Molly's parents enacted their own boundaries at the sake of their daughters, and even, her employers. While it is completely fair for Molly's parents to have that rule within their own home, and it was completely within Molly's right to find ways to circumvent the problem and attempt to find a solution; Molly's parents were also creating an impossible situation by not being flexible, when they were the ones who created the inflexible scenario by changing the dinner to be earlier and enforcing their rule.

Now, on the flip side, Molly also did something wrong. She turned off her phone and did what her parents wanted to please them. As will be discussed in a later chapter, wanting to please your parents is fine, but if it is at the cost of your own boundary—or even a boundary that may supersede family at certain times, like work—then there is an unhealthy atmosphere and a definite problem.

Workplace and family boundaries will specifically be discussed in a later chapter but it is imperative to understand : Your boundaries are your own and no one else's. That means they should be respected at all times, but that you should not enforce your own at the sake of others.

No Boundaries

Having a hopefully pretty good understanding of what healthy boundaries—and yours in particular—are beginning to look like, it is time to discuss what having no boundaries looks like.

Remember

If anytime during this section you notice uncomfortable similarities, do not be ashamed or worry. We will work through all of this together, and you are becoming more aware. Write down any similarities you notice, and together in a later chapter, we will tackle how to fix it (you may already be getting a basic idea on how to do that now anyways).

Essentially, having no boundaries looks like someone who constantly refuses to acknowledge that they might be the problem. Sounds a bit harsh, right? There are definitely times when it is completely not your fault or problem that something has gone wrong; and this is in no way, an accusation of you saying you should take on the responsibility of something that is not yours.

However, if you are constantly complaining that you feel like people are taking advantage of you, or are overstepping your personal boundaries constantly, it is time to take an honest look at your situation. Yes, there are definitely toxic environments where your boundaries would not be acknowledged or respected, but that is not what this section is discussing.

Often, people with no boundaries are highly aware of what boundaries are, they are just unwilling to acknowledge that part of having boundaries is accepting their personal responsibility to communicate and uphold them regularly. And on the one hand, that is totally relatable because doing so is a lot of work. The problem is that by shirking that responsibility, you are actually creating uncomfortable environments for the people you lash out at when they unknowingly step on your boundaries. Which, to be honest (and you can probably see where this is going), is going to lead to a big old mess with personal relationships. Boundaries are part of what makes personal relationships go round; because it helps people intrinsically understand how to interact around you. Not having any or—better yet—not defining them to yourself and others, is going to ensure eternal conflict.

Having no boundaries that are explicitly stated, or even subconsciously enforced by your words or actions, really does the exact opposite of what you want. Since no one understands what you want or what your own responsibilities are, they will trample all over you while trying to make you and everyone else happy. Which will not only annoy and upset you, but will also create a very messy interpersonal environment for everyone who interacts with you.

Consider this example: You and a friend decide to meet up and get some type of dessert. You mention wanting to get ice cream, and they neither confirm nor deny that that is what they want. So, you pick them up and take them to the ice cream store. Only, once you arrive, your friend gets upset and mentions that the entire time, they wanted to get cake.

While this example sounds a little ridiculous, it was your friend's duty to chime in with their own opinions and wants, and that by not doing so, they deliberately ignored their own wants and boundaries. However, asking them what they might have wanted rather than just assuming could have helped, as well. Yes, calling getting cake instead of ice cream a boundary seems ridiculous, but remember the chapter so far? Your boundaries are what you are responsible for or not, including what you want or not. Therefore, if your friend wanted cake, it was their responsibility to mention this want to you when you asked what they wanted to get to eat. Them not speaking up is first of all, not your fault, and second, their own problem and lack of boundaries.

Small Note

Before going any further it is important to recognize one key difference for any type of boundary, whether it be personal, familial, or professional. If you are in a toxic environment of any sort, no matter how hard you try to enforce or even state your boundaries, they will not be acknowledged on any level.

There is a huge difference between attempting to establish your boundaries with those around you, and having them willfully ignored—between not establishing anything yet still being upset. In the above example, your friend never told you her boundary and want, and as such, the situation became miserable.

On the flip side, if you attempt to state your boundaries to those around you, and no one acknowledges it, and you—understandably—become frustrated; that is a completely different kettle of fish.

Not having boundaries is very, very different from having your boundaries ignored. And that distinction is something that you will have to sit and think about at the end of this chapter (do not worry, there is a journal prompt to remind you).

Journaling

As mentioned in the Introduction, this is the time where some hard-thought truths should be discussed, and a lot of them have been indicated in this chapter so far. To sum it up, take a few moments to sit and think about what has been discussed, as well as a few other probing questions, to get the ball rolling on your own personal boundary journey.

First, begin to write down what you think your personal boundaries might be. Really consider every area of your life and what the big 'no's are in each scenario.

Second, take a look at your communication and understanding so far. Are you willing and ready to communicate your boundaries to those that need to know? If not, take a few minutes and think about why. Is it because you are afraid they will lash out at you? Or that you will get a negative reputation by standing up for your boundaries? If so, finish the journal prompts and continue onto the next chapter (really, you should read the rest anyway, but that was just a great segue).

Third, look at instances where you have felt like your boundaries were ignored. Ask yourself, did you properly communicate your boundary? Did you remind that person in that scenario of your boundary? If you did, journal down your thoughts and feelings along with the specific way that that person ignored your boundaries. Identifying their habits and ticks when they ignore boundaries will help you confront them about it later.

If you were not honest in communicating your boundaries, begin to think of ways that you could for when the next situation pops up. Also, and this one might hurt: be prepared to apologize if you did, and recognize that you acted disproportionately to the scenario because no one was aware of your boundaries; while they did cross your boundary line, it is really hard for them to be careful of something they are not aware of.

CHAPTER 2

Boundary Myths

Now that you have an idea of what boundaries look like, it is time to discuss what they are *not*, particularly the myths or misunderstandings surrounding boundaries. Please note, that while the word 'myth' is being used here, it is being used to note the false and very far-reaching lack of connection between what the myths are, and how boundaries work.

Unfortunately, boundaries have gotten a bit of a bad reputation, and this is predominantly due to people either reacting poorly to having someone else's boundaries being upheld, or the result of badly used boundaries, such as not being consistent or using boundaries as an excuse for something else.

This chapter will look at boundary myths in two ways: First, we will explain what the myths are, how they work, and possible answers as to why these myths might be in your own life. Second, this chapter will then deal with myth reconsiderations, or ways to re-think these negatives, so that your boundaries going forward will not be hindered by this type of negativity.

While reading through this chapter you may begin to notice some uncomfortable similarities to your own behaviors, habits, or beliefs. And while it will be a bit awkward, embrace those feelings and write them down. Noting where you see similarities between yourself and the following myths are going to be a key component to helping you begin to enact healthier boundaries in your life and relationships. While noting these similarities will be difficult, do not be too hard on yourself. Sadly these myths are perpetuated through misunderstanding and well-guided harmful mindsets. It is your job to think about how the myths are entrenched in your life, why they might be, and how you can confront those behaviors and mindsets going forward in your journey.

Boundary Myths and Reconsiderations

Alright, so, first of all, let's discuss how these myths, or bad mindsets, even came into being. How does something so 'simple' and 'easy' as boundaries get so messed up? Well, unfortunately, that answer is simple: because boundaries are so personal. While they may be easy in some cases to identify (and definitely become easy the more accustomed we are to being attuned to ourselves, wants, desires and responsibilities), this inner understanding and attunement is often where we begin to let the boundary myths come into play. This is done specifically, through the blurring between the lines of what we may believe are our responsibilities, or inner gut feelings of what a boundary is, versus the actuality of what our boundaries are. What makes these misunderstandings even worse is our lack of communication around these boundaries and the insistence on them being constantly honored.

You can spend as much time as you want on defining and understanding your boundaries—which you really should—but if you are unwilling to put the same amount of effort into communicating them and being firm on why your boundaries are what they are, then you will still allow little cracks in your mind for boundary myths to seep in. Particularly when enacting or explaining them.

But what if you are uncertain of your boundaries? For many of us, some of our most intrinsic core beliefs and boundaries are so fundamentally ingrained that we are unaware they even exist, which then makes properly communicating or explaining them not only confusing to ourselves, but also to those around us. Which is why communication is key to healthy boundaries. Nonetheless, good and clear communication is something that many people avoid, do not use, or are unsure of how to use and thus, bad boundaries are created, which in turn perpetuates the problem of boundary myths.

When it comes to our own lives and relationships the myths which will be discussed in this chapter are often enacted through our own misconceptions of how boundaries are portrayed, or are shown through someone we are in relationship with, because they have seen poor boundaries enacted.

Now, if you are someone who has let these myths perpetuate how you enact boundaries, do not worry, and do not let guilt or any type of negative emotion eat away at you. Awareness and open communication will lead the way, and throughout the rest of this book, we will delve into these myths and how to confront them in your thoughts and actions. On the other hand, if you know someone who has experienced these myths and are then projecting the end result of that onto you, make use of your connection to them and discuss it openly and nonjudgmentally. Talking through your boundaries and helping them understand how they will work with you will do marvels in helping to ease another person's fears.

But also remember: There are always going to be times when someone is terrified and/or attempts to resist your implementation of boundaries onto their relationship with you.

Yes, it sucks. Big time.

In a perfect world, we would all respect each other's boundaries and this book would not even be needed. However, we are human, and sadly that is not yet the case. Therefore, while enacting and enforcing your own boundaries is commendable and highly encouraged, it also comes with the possibility of creating poor reactions in some people. If you remember the Introduction and previous chapter, this is where the personal responsibility and honestly, overall goal of your boundaries, comes in. Having and enforcing your boundaries are mainly for yourself, with the happy side-effect of being healthy for those around you. But it is not the other way around. Do not forget this when going forward with the rest of the chapters, and specifically, when looking and confronting these boundary myths.

Small Note

Before going into the myths, there are two things you should note. First, for this chapter, what you need to begin to understand is that confronting these myths will help you in practicing your boundaries; not necessarily in helping other people understand, respect, or even acknowledge that your boundaries exist. Second, to properly use this chapter, read through the definitions of each myth, the examples, and then the ways that the reconsiderations work in each of the examples.

If any of these things relate to you, take a moment—even grab a highlighter or adjust your ebook reader to make notes, if you have to—to really sit down and analyze those particular examples, what resonates with you, and how it can be battled in your own life.

So, without further ado, let's begin!

Selfishness & Guilt

In all honesty, selfishness and guilt are both the easiest and most complicated forms of boundary myths for several reasons. First, selfishness and guilt play into each other, as both of the emotions—and the triggers of those emotions—tend to coincide. Second, these are two of the most common socially enforced backlashes from when people attempt to begin implementing healthy boundaries in their relationships. Third, both guilt and selfishness have this fine line of being a valid accusation towards you when you enact your boundaries, versus the social enforcement of those feelings for even implementing boundaries.

If that sounded a little too confusing, do not worry, just keep reading. It will all make sense soon, promise.

The Myth of Selfishness

A popular concept that stops many people from wanting to begin implementing boundaries is that doing so would make them seem selfish. Sadly, the birth of this myth could come from anywhere, and to make matters worse, there is a bit of truth to this statement. With the myth of selfishness, there is this uncomfortable reality that, at times, implementing your boundaries will be selfish.

The general understanding of selfishness is that you are either thinking or performing actions without a care for the consequences it could have on others. You are only concerned about yourself and what you need or want. And on the one hand, boundaries should never really get to the extreme of that point—which is where you use your boundaries at the cost or detriment of another person. But… What if it does?

There are definitely going to be times when your boundaries could come at the cost of another human; the difference is that these moments should be extenuating circumstances, rather than daily occurrences. For instance, take the extreme example of you being a witness in a trial for a crime. Your innermost boundary (hopefully) is to be honest with what you saw, even if that incriminates someone who did wrong. Situations like this are not a bad time to be selfish with your boundaries. In fact, many would argue that that is not even being selfish, you are being a law-abiding citizen.

So then, why do people view boundaries as selfish? Let's look at it another way: boundaries are a tricky thing, because they are intrinsically built to ensure your own mental health and safety; and it merely benefits those around you, because you are choosing to be a safer and better person. You cannot help others when you are too tired, emotionally drained, or unable to help because you lack the boundaries to take a step back and care for yourself. The problem is, this entire concept of saying 'no' becomes that really messy area where some people's perspectives view that 'no' is selfish. And honestly, it can be. But if used and said properly, 'no' should not be seen in a negative or bad way.

Saying 'no' is something we learn early on in childhood, because we know that the word will stop an action we do not want, need, or like. Why has this become a problem in our adult lives? Because in modern society we have let politeness dictate that we are often unable to say 'no', which is a shame and not incredibly healthy, because it is causing us to forget that 'no' is a basic boundary we need to enact. Now, there is a difference between saying 'no' because it is a specific boundary or you need that particular time, compared to always saying 'no', which will be covered later on in this chapter.

However, if you are saying 'no' to seemingly harmless things like coffee with a friend occasionally, then you are not being selfish by enacting your own boundaries. You cannot help anyone before you help yourself. Therefore, putting yourself last will help no one. If your 'no' is met with "you are being selfish" there is a good chance that the person who said that is not honoring your boundaries, and to watch them carefully. Take a look at the following example:

Over the past few years, you have been noticing that your social battery has been going down. You are more tired than before, and planning events for your different activities has become more of a chore than an enjoyable past-time. On the advice of a friend, you begin to keep a journal of your feelings for each event over a period of several months. During that time, you notice that the main drain on your time, social energy and overall life, is a club where you are the main organizer and chief volunteer. However, this is your longest and most dearest volunteer position, so you begin to become more vocal for several events on how you need the other volunteers' help, with little success. Even implementing their mandatory attendance has done little to help ease all of the work that you end up doing. So, you decide that to combat the social burnout, you are going to step down from being the chief organizer and doer of everything. While the decision is hard, you recognize that this is the only way to ensure that the rest of your social life does not suffer. However, when you tell your fellow volunteers your plan and 'exit' (you are not fully leaving, you are just no longer being the main person they all come to for help), their responses are less than pleasant. Some called you 'selfish' and others asked how the club could possibly run without you. For context, none of those other volunteers had put in nearly half of the time you have over the last year, at the very minimum.

Reconsidering Selfishness

There are several things to note in the above example. First, the decision to step down was not a rash or impulsive decision. It was done with methodical care and deep soul-searching to ensure it was what you wanted and needed. Second, you did attempt to resolve the lack of boundaries with how the other volunteers treated the club and you. While there is the argument that you could have gone farther, let's say that for that argument's sake, in several meetings you did explicitly say "I need more help," and nothing changed. Rcsigning as the head volunteer was your last resort.

Second, this decision was made to save yourself—therefore, it was a decision based on a personal boundary and the emotional intelligence of understanding what you needed to do to maintain the rest of your life. If you ever notice that something in your life becomes all-encompassing, when that is never what it should be, there is absolutely nothing wrong with taking a step back from it (please note that this is referring to activities, jobs, or non-familial based relationships) . While it is cliche, there is a reason that so many people say, "it's your life," because it is. You get to decide where you spend your time, energy, and so on; and if any of those decisions become too much, and you feel that your own mental, emotional, or even physical health are being put on the line for that position, then something is wrong.

Third, consider how people reacted to your stepping down. For enacting the final thing you can do to save your own mental health and overall well-being, you are essentially being called selfish. Yet, remember, that none of these people had not stepped up to the plate when you repeatedly asked for more help in the past few months. You explicitly stated that you needed help. You gave the others a chance to step up and help you. Now, they will have to pay the consequences for not honoring your boundary or listening to your needs.

In this example, stepping down does not hurt anyone, does not put anyone else's boundaries or health at risk, and it is certainly not jeopardizing a common goal that the group has been striving for. In the example you are not not being a team player; you are putting a stop to being a one-man team.

If, however, you are still unsure, here are a few sure-fire ways your boundaries are being selfish—in a bad way.

First, is when your boundaries cause you to never be available to others. Yes, you should protect yourself, and you are completely within your right to tell someone that you do not have the emotional availability—in that particular moment—to help them. But if you are doing that all the time, then you are using boundaries to avoid being a good friend or family member, because unless there is something deeply wrong (where you should really seek professional help), there should be a time when you are able to help someone else. If you are still unsure, think about group projects, or work. Is there one team member who uses boundaries as an excuse to never really participate in the team? They never stay late, they never socialize, and they never help more than the bare minimum? Yes, having boundaries about the work/life balance are important—do not misunderstand that particular point. It is how that person uses boundaries to ensure that they are never part of the culture, and to not work hard, that is the problem (Mort, 2021).

Second, is when you are using your boundaries to control other people (this does not count if you are the parents of young children, or specific instances which will be covered in a later chapter). What this means is when you use your boundary to ensure that someone else does not have their personal freedom. Consider the difference between these two statements: "Due to my religious preferences, I do not eat pork," versus, "Since I do not eat pork, you should not serve or eat it in my presence either," (Mort, 2021). In the first one, the person is politely stating what they will not eat, but are allowing everyone else in the setting to do as they wish. In the second, the person is blatantly expecting everyone else to bow down to their own boundary while at that event.

Notice the subtle difference?

Small Note

Your boundaries should never be formed to hurt another human. If you are beginning to think that someone else's 'boundaries' are hurting you, find a safe person or therapist to talk that over. Keep a journal of instances where those boundaries are used and your feelings about them, to begin keeping record. Make sure they do not have access to that journal.

The Myth of Guilt

Guilt is probably one of the biggest and perhaps the worst of all the myths surrounding boundaries, because it is one of the most subtle forms of emotions we encounter. There are quite a few times, even in adulthood, where many of us feel guilty over something and we either cannot quite name what it is, or we are unsure if that guilt is even justified. Additionally, many people—maybe even you—are pre-programmed to feel guilty when instigating healthy boundaries; and this could be for a plethora of reasons. Perhaps it is because you feel guilty for putting that type of expectation on a loved one. Perhaps it is because you feel guilty for being selfish. Guilt has this very bad habit of tacking itself onto almost everything and anything, and what is worse, it allows bad behaviors to continue because we bow to the shame it induces.

Have you ever felt the shame of guilt? It is not pretty, and even if that shame and guilt are undeserved, it is incredibly hard to fight. Now add all of those complex emotions on top of instigating boundaries, and it is no wonder that this is a key way many people are able to get in the way of others' establishing their own boundaries, or why some people have a hard time coming up with their own boundaries.

Remember

You should never feel guilty for implementing and standing firm to your own boundaries. Your boundaries are essentially your way of saying what you are willing to be responsible for or not. Ergo, there has been some type of thought (even if it is subconscious) about what you can or cannot handle. Therefore, if you cannot handle something in that particular moment, unless there are extenuating circumstances (which will be covered in the next chapter), you are not at fault for putting your mental and physical health first by enacting your own boundaries.

Going back to understanding how guilt works with your boundaries, or, more specifically, how it ruins your boundaries, let's discuss what happens when someone or something is done to make you feel guilty for defending or using your boundaries.

For instance, Margaret had never really enforced her own boundaries with friends before, but after plucking up some courage, she decided to start. This began with her friend, Tom, who would often well-meaningly buy Margaret a cup of coffee. Margaret would always feel this subconscious pressure to buy Tom a coffee or something else, in return. After thinking it over, and looking at life circumstances which had changed her finances, Margaret began to realize that this was her own lack of boundaries and communication; so the next time she got together with Tom, she asked him to not buy her a cup of coffee, as she could not afford to buy him a treat or pay him back. In response, Tom showed up at Margaret's with his own coffee and nothing else. While on their outing, Tom asked Margaret if buying the coffee had made her uncomfortable, and Margaret told him about her financial difficulties and how she could not afford to reciprocate Tom's generosity. Tom responded with an, "Oh, I did not know you felt that way when I brought you coffee, I am sorry, that was not my intention." By saying this, Tom was able to signal to Margaret that her feelings of needing to reciprocate Tom's generosity were completely her own and in no way actually projected onto her by Tom.

Now, compare that example to the following:

Compared to Tom, Margaret was also beginning to stand up to her sister Julie. Julie always had this knack of trying to one-up her presents. If Margaret got Julie earrings,

Julie got Margaret a necklace, and the escalation would continue. However, for the time being, those types of gifts were no longer something Margaret could afford; and Julie was aware of that. So, when Julie's birthday rolled around, Margaret got Julie a beautiful—but simple—bracelet. It was very pretty and dainty, but definitely not the one-up style that the sisters had become known for. While Julie was thankful for the gift, Margaret could tell that Julie was not as excited about this one, as when Margaret had received a watch for her own birthday. Feeling guilty about the disparity, Margaret bought a sweater—which she could not really afford—for Julie the following day, which her sister received very, very happily.

Reconsidering Guilt

Notice the difference between the two examples. In the first, Tom quickly made Margaret realize that her guilt was unnecessary, and that his gifts and time were not something Margaret had to feel guilty, or obligated, to return. In comparison, Margaret's sister Julie did not do the same. In fact, she subtly encouraged Margaret's guilt over gifts—which could have been subconscious—resulting in Margaret bowing down to her guilt and getting Julie something she could not afford.

Now, there are two things to learn from this example.

First: All relationships do have this subconscious give-and-take mentality. If you are constantly putting way more effort into any relationship than the other person, then there is an imbalance of priorities and you need to address that. It could either be you stepping back, or talking with that friend. On the other hand, this give-and-take is natural and normal in relationships, and is honestly something that should stay in place. This section is definitely not telling you to follow Margaret's example with Tom and to take his gifts and give nothing in return. There is a time and place for everything, and as you will note, in this example it was specifically mentioned that Margaret could not afford it at that time. This is a temporary boundary Margaret has in place to protect herself, and Tom is aware of that and respects it. However, that is not to say that you should begin to enforce a tit for tat mentality. Simply pay attention and ensure that you are not feeling like you are being taken advantage of (or make sure you are not the one taking advantage of the other person) when it comes to time, gifts, or money in relationships, while also understanding the dynamic of that relationship (e.g., do not hold your parents or relatives to the same standard as friends, etc.).

Second: Both of these examples involved money, because money is something that most people feel guilty about intrinsically when there is an imbalance. However, this could be anything, like time spent, or even how emotionally attentive the other person is in comparison to you.

The biggest takeaway you can get when it comes to guilt and boundaries is to look at the intention of the person behind them, and how that person reacts when you subtly shift, or enforce, your own boundaries. Gifts, which include time, items, and emotions, should be given freely, and if they are not, there is a good indicator that the feelings of obligation you have towards that relationship, are a lack of boundaries (Cloud & John Sims Townsend, 2002).

Again, this statement does not involve the natural give and take of a relationship, but it is a clue to beginning to consider your emotions in relationships. If you feel guilty or beholden to certain relationships because they did something for you, you need to sit down and think about why you feel this guilt, and what would happen if you alleviated it by not doing that action, or shifting that action to fit your boundaries better. If the other person is upset by this shift, then there is a lack of boundary understanding you need to address. However, if they go with the flow and do not get upset by that shift, and honor it, then the guilt was an innermost projection.

When it comes to reconsidering guilt, there are two obstacles that have to be faced. First, there is a personal element to the emotion of guilt, because at some point or another, it is something that you not only feel, but may in fact, place onto yourself as well. Good news is that this is one of the easiest to combat on a daily basis. Notice that the phrase says 'easy' not 'enjoyable' or any synonym with that intention. Guilt is easy to combat because there are hundreds of mantras out there to help you fight it on a daily basis. You could make it a screensaver, find an audio/podcast reminder, even set some type of message alert on your phone to go off 'x' amount of times a day, to remind you that you do not need to feel guilty for being healthy with your personal boundaries and to improve your life. On top of that, the majority of the modern world is interested in fighting the guilt many feel when creating healthy boundaries. So not only are there quite a few tools to help you, but the majority of people are actually on your side of helping you combat it as well.

The second thing to reconsider with guilt is that you will be combating more than just a person's own beliefs. Many guilt-based myths surrounding boundaries come from cultural, generational, and personal beliefs surrounding boundaries. Which means that you have to be in top-form to continuously fight it, as well as have a clear understanding of where the implication of guilt is coming from. Or, in other words, why is someone trying to make you feel guilty over your boundaries?

Remember the examples: Julie's enforced guilt onto Margaret was because she was accustomed to getting certain types of gifts from her sister, and was unwilling to accept the financial changes in Margaret's life and the hindrance it would put on her expectations. In comparison, Tom had no guilt put onto Margaret for the change in their routine.

When it comes to Julie, the guilt she subtly enforced onto her sister was based simply out of historical familial expectations—which is something many of us have probably experienced. These are sometimes the hardest forms of guilt-inducing actions to fight, because many people love their family and traditions dearly. In these scenarios, you will need to just grit your teeth and ride out the guilt by saying a mantra continuously in your head. There is really no other easy fix for it.

Selfishness and Guilt Roundup

This particular section has a lot of information pertaining to guilt and shame, which is why it is so long and there are so many sub-categories. Just in case you have any lingering doubts or confusion, here is a brief summation of this segment.

First, selfishness and guilt are more commonly attached to boundaries than we like to think.

Second, you are never selfish, nor should you feel guilty, for enacting healthy boundaries in unhealthy scenarios. If you are putting others before yourself continuously, there will be a time when you are no longer going to be helpful to anyone, and that is not the result anyone wants. There may be times when you are genuinely being selfish by putting yourself first and not saying yes to everything everyone asks of you. And that is okay.

Third, both selfishness and guilt do have the small potential of being valid accusations if you are enacting or using your boundaries improperly towards others, or badly in situations. For instance, if you are using boundaries to avoid doing something, which could end up being harmful or put more work onto other people who also have strong boundaries, then there is a problem.

Fourth, guilt is toxic and somehow attaches itself to everything that is healthy, mainly because it can come from a variety of relatively understandable reasons. That does not mean that you should let any projected guilt influence how you enact your boundaries. Thankfully, there are many options on how to fight guilt, so you are not lacking help or resources to begin picking and choosing what will work for you.

Myth: Some Relationships Do Not Need Them

Another myth with boundaries is the concept that some people believe they are exempt from your boundaries. To be honest, there may very well be times when these people are, but not for the reasons they think. Those situations are very rare and are for short periods of time, like with newborn babies. It is pretty impossible—and actually really dangerous—to tell a newborn that you have to put yourself first before you feed or change them, without a backup helper in place. If you have someone to help you, then go for it (and honestly, all new mothers should have some type of help for moments like this), but if that help is not there, taking that time and leaving a newborn unattended when they need attention (e.g., they are crying for something) is not the best of ideas. Extenuating, or life phase circumstances, such as: emergencies, newborns, elderly, or those with memory retention problems or special needs, are really the only times that someone should not have boundaries put on them. Mostly because these scenarios encompass situations where your boundaries, while important, cannot simply be enacted at the drop of a hat. You need more preparation and help to do them, simply because these situations are where someone else is depending on you entirely.

Or, on the other hand, there are some people in your life where certain boundaries may never actually affect them, so they may be unaware of that particular boundary. For instance, it is pretty rare for a family member to know a specific, non-generic boundary you have in dating (such as your personal boundaries on physical touch), unless you have discussed your romantic life in detail.

But what about those people who tell you that your relationship with them does not need boundaries?

In all honesty, that is a massive problem, and something that needs to be addressed immediately in your relationship with them. Thankfully, most people are terrified of boundaries due to the lack of communication that often surrounds them, so if you are able to sit down with the person and discuss why they think they are exempt from your boundaries, you may be able to resolve the problem. Or, you may now know exactly why they think they are exempt and decide what to do from there.

A great example would be between Anthony and his cousin Mark. The two had grown up together and were very close, almost like brothers. However, as they began to get older, things got… interesting. The biggest problem Anthony was beginning to face was Mark's newfound belief that his knowledge was the only knowledge that was good, therefore many of Anthony's opinions were ignored or called ignorant or stupid. While Anthony was willing to admit that some of his opinions were a little half-done and were not all well researched or set in stone, they were only teenagers, and there was definitely time for him to learn and sort them out. So, having had enough, Anthony decided to confront Mark. The problem is that the confrontation did not go well. In response to Anthony mentioning that he did not feel like he was being respected, which is a generic and rudimentary boundary, Mark laughed it off and said to Anthony: "Well, it is a good thing we are family, right? Guess that does not really apply to me!"

While on the one hand Mark has a tiny point, as most family members have a special relationship with boundaries (which will be covered in the next chapter), he has got one thing absolutely wrong. Just because someone is family does not mean that they are exempt from your boundaries, or that they do not have to respect them.

No one is exempt from your boundaries, aside from the specific instances which were mentioned earlier.

On the flip side, there could be the potential that you personally think some relationships are exempt from your boundaries. You are not going to like this, but you are wrong. Oh, so, so, wrong. Every relationship—aside from the above exemptions—needs boundaries. You may not like enacting them. You may not be sure about what they look like. But that relationship needs them.

Reconsidering Relationships

When it comes to reconsidering how this myth might have gotten into your life, it painfully starts with the question of who did you allow to walk over your boundaries, because that person was too important to you to lose? The answers to this could be endless. It could be a close family member who guilt-trips you, it could be your own guilt-enforced belief that you cannot, or should not, be firm with that particular person (notice that theme here? How guilt walked right on over from its above segment into here? See, it is one of the most prevalent anti-boundary things in existence). You know what? That's totally understandable, it is scary to set a boundary with someone who blatantly disrespects them, but is still so important to you. Yes, it does happen, and it very well might have happened to you. However, you need to set boundaries. Every relationship needs them.

Your boundaries are what you can or cannot handle, and that includes those around you. That includes those family members, that childhood best friend, your romantic partner, your boss, or coworkers. The guilt you are feeling over including them in the list of people you need to have boundaries with is either through them, or projected from them by yourself. Either way, you need to confront that guilt, because without boundaries in those relationships, you are not going to have a good, healthy, or thriving relationship.

Myth: Boundaries Push People Away

Some people are truly afraid of you putting boundaries on them, because they noticed that people previously used that as a reason to distance their relationship.

Some people use very legitimate and healthy boundaries on a person who does not have, want, or understand those types of boundaries, and therefore while the boundaries are respected, the relationship still dwindles. These things happen, whether it is because of enforcing boundaries or not. There are probably quite a few of you reading this who are suddenly remembering that friend they once talked to, that you have not heard from in some time. The problem then, is that sometimes, the statement of enforcing your boundaries to that friend, and then the consequent dwindling of the friendship, brings up this nasty correlation which was completely unintentional. However, depending on how those boundaries were specifically stated and enforced, it makes sense that some people are genuinely afraid that boundaries will mean they would lose you as a friend. If this is what you think is happening, then honestly, talk to that friend. If this is a relationship you want to keep, find ways to work through their fear with them, while they also learn to respect your boundaries.

The person who is going to be denied access to you by your boundaries is throwing a small little tantrum over the change in the relationship, mainly because they are frustrated that their control is taken away.

Maybe you are afraid of enforcing boundaries, because you believe it will push people away. Similar to the types of examples and scenarios discussed above, it is completely reasonable to be afraid that some of your boundaries will scare the ones you are closest to away. But in reality, that should not happen.

Reconsidering Pushing

Reconsidering the framing of the above situations should be relatively easy and brief, so here we go.

For the situation where a friendship naturally dwindled but it appeared like boundaries were the main cause, as mentioned earlier, communication is a good remedy to fix that. Talking it through with a friend, or even talking your fears and boundaries through with that person, will ease a lot of fear, guilt, and lack of desire to continue on your boundary journey. If the person is willing, the two of you could even come up with ways to stop both of your fears together. This could be something like having a code word you could both add to a text message, or being okay with over communication. Thankfully, resolving this first fear is easy, once you get past the awkward first bit of discussing your fears.

We mentioned the situation wherein someone else is throwing a tantrum because they lost control over you, and this can be difficult to address, but you must do so anyway. So, call them out on it. Calling out someone who is intrinsically manipulating you is hard because you are not just confronting the unknown of what could happen to your relationship, you are confronting someone who is used to controlling and manipulating you; which means that the conversation could go sideways and you are back at square one. A great fix for this is to bring a safe, neutral, third party (like one of your safe people) who would be able to see through the manipulator's tactics. You could even use that safe person continuously as a fact checker if you decide to stay in contact with that other relationship. Never underestimate the joy and ease of having safe people in your life.

When people are afraid that your boundaries will push them away, here are a few thoughts to keep you going: First, some people may respect your boundaries and while the relationship will shift, it will still exist. Not everyone who is bad at enforcing their own boundaries will drop those that are good at enforcing their own. There is a chance for the relationship to sort itself out once the natural understanding of the new limits has happened. Second, if the person is like the second example above, then in all honesty, who needs them? The people who used your lack of boundaries to control you are not people you need in your life anyways. Same goes for those who are upset with your boundaries because it inconveniences them.

Your boundaries are for your health, and if someone cannot respect or encourage you on that journey, you do not need them.

Small Note

This does not necessarily include the people who have such a bad understanding of boundaries that they panic when you begin to instate them in your relationship. If someone reacts to your boundaries out of fear, try to talk to them about it one-on-one.

If you think or notice someone is acting differently after you tell them about your boundaries, ask them what is going on. If they are honest with you, chances are, you will be able to work it out.

However, if they use your boundaries as a reason to bring up why they should be the exception, or that your boundary is unnecessary, then stop and leave. Just because you are willing to communicate does not mean you can open the door to manipulation or guilt-tripping. Been there, done that, we are not going back.

Myth: Boundaries Are a Sign of Rudeness

Honestly, it makes sense that some people view setting and enforcing boundaries as a sign of rudeness. Depending on your generational, cultural, or even societal background, certain things that some people view as boundaries were maybe not as optional for them when they were forming a sense of identity and intrinsic boundaries. For instance, if someone is vegetarian, but goes to a cultural home and cannot eat half the food, it creates an awkward situation as most cultures view not eating their food as rude, however, the vegetarian's rudimentary dietary boundary is to not eat meat. In this type of scenario, it is best to forewarn the host of any dietary issues, or find a way to bring it up in conversation before the event.

Now that the exception is out of the way, time to confront the people who view your boundaries as being rude. Aside from cultural, generational, or societal implications like the above example, there is never a time when your boundaries are rude. How you enforce them might be. How you explicitly confront people who ignore them might be. But you setting them will never be.

Reconsidering Rude

If you personally feel like you are being rude when you are setting your boundaries, take a moment to consider why that might be. Is it because of how you worded it? If so, go back over that dialogue in your head and really ask yourself if you were being rude, or if you are projecting guilt onto yourself. If you are projecting, remind yourself that setting boundaries is to ensure that you are creating a safe environment for yourself.

Now, if someone called you rude, it is time to confront the elephant in the room. That person is most likely being a bit of a boundary bully. Chances are, they do not like what that boundary does to them personally, and are trying to guilt trip you into backing down. Do not let them. Stand firm. This is not the time or place to bow down to their wishes.

Another question to ask yourself: Could your behavior be construed as rude because you used nonverbal cues (this will be covered later), like excluding yourself from certain scenarios, or avoiding certain people? If you are doing those things and again, the rudeness is self-projected, then it is time for you to recognize a learning curve with boundaries. There will be times when enacting your boundaries will feel rude because you are excusing yourself from situations where you previously ensured you gutted through it. Leaving, ignoring, or being not entirely present (like being on your phone) in those scenarios is not a bad thing. You are silently, or vocally, enforcing your boundaries. As long as you ensure that you are being respectful, you are good to go.

Now, if you are confronted by someone, it is time to remind them of your boundaries and how those specific scenarios are encroaching on them. If they react poorly, then you know who will not respect your boundaries going forward.

Always Saying "No"

This section will have many similarities to the selfishness segment, but it is still worth discussing on its own. The word 'no' is something that most of us know and respect since childhood. Yet when it comes to boundaries this word is a bit of a *Goldie Locks* situation. Some people never use it, some people use it too often, and others use it just enough. The problem is figuring out what your personal balance for the use of 'no' actually is. Especially since there is a bit of a tricky discrimination between finding what your boundaries are versus either your lack of boundaries, poor communication, or inconsideration towards others (Virro, 2020).

Before your worst fears get a hold of you, let's walk this through. Setting boundaries means ensuring that you take time to care for yourself and listen to your body when it is telling you that you need to slow down, take a break, or that certain environments are not healthy for you to be in. Think of them as a meter for what you can or cannot do in that particular scenario/life phase. Therefore, on that premise, saying 'no' is actually not that unhealthy.

Armed with that knowledge, let's go through the three types of boundary 'no's again.

The first scenario is those who never use the word. This is actually a lack of boundaries and is very dangerous, as it can cause fatigue, social exhaustion, burnout, and even cause you to be seen as unreliable towards your commitments. Sounds crazy? Take a moment to think about it. It is very likely that you know someone who takes on way too much for their plate. Perhaps they volunteer at too many events, have too many part-time jobs, or say 'yes' to every social event and then are only at each event for half an hour in order to make it everywhere. The majority of people who never say 'no' tend to fall into the people pleasing category; as they are trying to make everyone happy, but are only making themselves, and everyone else, miserable. Some of you are probably thinking: "That's not true! They are the life of the party!"

While this sounds a bit pessimistic… They are the life of the party… for now. Sooner or later their calendar will catch up to them and then they will begin dropping everything like hot pies without an oven mitt.

So, then, how is this actually breaking personal boundaries? On the surface, it may not seem like it, unless you actually have begun a boundary where you will not take on more than you can do. However, this mindset is dangerous for two reasons. The first is that most people expect you to show up when you commit to it. While your friends may be more annoyed at your constant tardiness or canceling; a job, on the other hand, will not be so forgiving. The second problem is when you look at this scenario a bit more closely. The definition of boundaries throughout this entire book is defined as understanding what is your responsibility or not, which then dovetails rather nicely into the entire balancing act of responsibilities versus freedoms versus expectations.

While that discussion is not going to be done here, it does bring up an interesting point of: If boundaries are essentially understanding what you are and are willing to be responsible for, then taking on too many things and not upholding any end of the bargain for any of the things you said you would, is essentially, not fulfilling that definition.

Small Note

This section is by no means saying that you can begin to be that person who simply drops everything at the last minute because your newfound boundary of saying 'no' must be respected. Just because boundaries involve you recognizing what you can or cannot handle, does not mean that you get to be irresponsible and drop everything last-minute. What this does mean is that you can talk to those above you and mention your struggles and together come up with solutions.

The second scenario is the overuse of the word 'no', which in all honesty, is just as bad as the first. Why? Because you are limiting your life a little too much. If you are saying 'no' often because of valid things like: you do not have time, you do not like those people, you do not like that event, then this is not a boundary issue, it is a social/time of life issue which you can either proactively change this week, or you can hope passes with time. However, there are other people who use the word 'no' all the time, and then are upset that they are either not invited to things, missed out on that event, or are afraid that they will not achieve everything they want to do.

Remember: There is a fine line between saying 'no' to respect your boundaries and your goals, and then using 'no' as an excuse to not get there. Do not let your 'no' be an excuse to not get there.

Reconsidering 'No'

The reconsidering of the word 'no' is the same as the third scenario: those who use it just enough, because it means that you have attained the balance of your boundaries and your wants. So, how do you get here? First of all, we need to stop viewing 'no' as this bad word. It is a great intrinsic sign that something is wrong and you need to change.

For instance, if you are the first example of 'no', or, you never use the word, that is a sign that you need to start using it more! The word will not hurt you, the action will not hurt you, and in fact, it may actually give you a tad more freedom. Now, if you absolutely live life full-on, pedal to the metal because you are afraid of missing out, or not being at that one absolutely crazy event, it is really time to think about your priorities and how you can make it all work.

This may seem counterintuitive for this segment, but it is absolutely possible for you to be able to do everything you want. You can be that healthy person who goes to the gym and still has a thriving social life. You can still be a student and work full time. You can still do all of these things and have a full and healthy family life.

So, how do you do it?

So glad you asked. You do it through boundaries!

If it was at all possible, there would be an insert of an evil kitten right above that line. Because having this full and thriving life is exactly what boundaries and open communication gets you. It enables you to set up the life you want, with very little backlash. Now, before you keep going the way you are now, remember: Boundaries include saying 'no'. It can be said with an absolute guarantee that those social media socialites who have and do it all, take time for themselves, say no to some events, and say no to some outings to ensure that everything gets done.

When used appropriately, 'no' will help you get the life you want, and yes, fight all of the innermost thoughts you are having right now about how that sounds wrong. Why? Because notice that the phrase included 'appropriately'. That does not mean you never use it, that does not mean you use it too much, that means you should use it just enough.

And how do you do that?

By understanding your boundaries and beginning to fight the negative connotations the word has. Instead, begin to reconsider 'no' as "not right now". It is amazing how simply changing the word, but keeping the connotation, makes a lot of the fears surrounding it less scary and all intrusive. Saying "not right now" does not mean you will never, or that you will stop. It simply means that for the time you were asked about, you have other plans.

So then, how do you go about ensuring that you use 'no' just enough, in a realistic way? Well, the first thing is to begin figuring out where you are not saying 'no 'enough. That could be anything from all of your life, to simply just your social outings. Identifying where you are unwilling or do not want to say 'no' will help you figure out why you are not willing to limit that area of your life. Once you know the why, you can then begin to combat it.

For instance, if you are limiting your social life because you are afraid that you will miss out on special events, then you can begin to logistically fight that belief by asking yourself how many of those events were actually memorable? Being realistic with your wants versus the reality of your life will help you begin to really see where your memory or hope is getting ahead of where your boundaries should be.

Now for the second scenario, where your 'no' is because you are afraid to leave your comfort zone. There is a big difference between something you intrinsically know is a physical boundary, such as not going on specific rides or doing certain adrenaline based things, and not allowing yourself to be pushed. Honestly, those boundaries are found by trial and error or a deep understanding of yourself and your limits. But, to say the old adage: How do you know if you do not try?

Now, that is not saying to go and bungee jump if you are not an adrenaline junkie or that was never something you wanted to do. And that is also not a green light to put yourself in dangerous scenarios. What this is saying is that if you are using your 'no' to not get to know new people, to not be social with team members, or to not even attempt new things, then perhaps you are using the word 'no' as a crutch.

To combat this, begin with tiny steps. Say 'yes' to that coffee with a friend or coworker that you have been maybe wanting to go to, but originally said 'no' to. Try that new biking trail with a friend. Book that vacation. It begins with the first small step.

Just remember: Do it safely and do it wisely. Do not suddenly become the 'yes' man and then have to re-learn how to instigate 'no' in a healthy way. Instead, learn to instigate 'yes' in a healthy way. Which is to intrinsically ask yourself why your first reaction is 'no'. Is it because that is your habit? Or because you do not want to?

Small Note

While this chapter is a bit of a back and forth mentality, remember this: Your 'no' is enough. Not wanting to go out with that person simply because you do not want to is enough.

When it comes to boundaries and the words 'no' and 'yes', it is a balancing act, but underneath all that balance needs to be this intrinsic understanding of what you do and do not want. Make sure that both your 'no' and 'yes' align with those wants. This will help you maintain and upkeep your boundaries while going to where you want to go and doing what you have always wanted to.

You can have and do it all, but you need your boundaries to get there.

Journaling

This chapter was a lot to take in, so re-reading it, or parsing over certain things that stuck out at you, or maybe did not make a lot of sense, will be important. This is not a sprint, it is a marathon, and the goal of this marathon is for you to understand and know your boundaries and be comfortable to enforce them in any situation you find yourself in. Part of that is to ensure that you understand these boundary myths and how to fight them in your own life and mind.

That being said, as mentioned previously, take a moment and go over the examples that really resonate with your own life. Write down instances where these myths have happened to you, and then begin to restructure and reconsider how you can handle those going forward.

If you are unsure if something is being done properly, find a safe person—or a licensed therapist—who can help guide you on the nuances of your own particular circumstances.

CHAPTER 3

How to Be More Assertive

Living a life with healthy boundaries includes knowing and understanding how to be assertive with your boundaries. Except, this is something that so many of us struggle with due to any of the previously mentioned myths about boundaries, personality conflicts with assertion, or even just our own confusion on how to be assertive without being rude.

The first thing that you need to know, before even discussing tactics for boundaries in particular, is that as long as you are respectful and polite in your words, and aware of the surroundings and audience you have, being assertive is never rude. It is being calmly and resiliently assured of what you are saying and not allowing peer pressure or bullying to cow you into changing your mind.

Which is all well and good as a statement, but how do you actually go through with it?

This chapter will deal exclusively with strategies you can implement to be more assertive when setting and enforcing your boundaries. You do not necessarily have to use all of them, but you should be able to find a combination that works for both you and your situations.

Strategies for Assertiveness with Boundaries

Asserting your boundaries seems daunting, but there are actually several incredibly practical and easy ways to go about it. Each of them will be discussed individually with examples on how you can begin being assertive, while polite, about your boundaries.

Communicate Your Boundaries

Aha, bet you thought we were done with discussing communication, but we are not. As has been mentioned multiple times throughout this book so far, communication is key in upholding and respecting your boundaries. Additionally, communication has this handy dandy little trick of ensuring that those you talk to respect your boundaries, while also putting your own mind and emotional intelligence on high alert as to whether you are actually doing what you said you would. But how do you actually communicate them to others? Well, there are two very obvious ways: either verbally or nonverbally.

Verbal Boundaries

Verbal boundaries are pretty clear and simple. They are the "I will" or "I will not" statements. The actual phrasing can change, but the intent is the same.

The problem then, with verbal boundaries, is not that they are being openly communicated, but whether you have done so in a respectful, clear, concise, and correct manner. Sounds a bit odd, right? How can boundaries fall into any of the above categories?

Well, boundaries actually go two ways. For your boundaries to be acknowledged and respected, you need to also respect other people's boundaries. And the foundation of this respect is through open and clear communication. How you communicate your boundaries will be the cornerstone of what you expect from others, and what you will or will not tolerate in how they treat them.

Clearly communicating your boundaries will ensure that no one misunderstands them, while also allowing your boundaries to remain fluid to accommodate and change with you, your life and the events and people around you. This also enables you to allow your boundaries to permeate different areas and relationships of your life. While our communication will vary depending on the circumstance, the actual boundary will often not change. For instance, your boundary of being respected is constant throughout every area of your life, but how you communicate that to your coworkers is probably really different from how you would communicate that to friends and family.

Which then brings up an important aspect of communicating boundaries: being polite versus cushioning our wants and needs. So often when we communicate our boundaries, we believe that we need to cushion them with too much politeness, correct phrasing, and unnecessary words to avoid hurting other people's feelings. Which is odd considering that we are discussing your personal boundaries. You know what? Your boundaries should technically never hurt someone's feelings (and if it does, that is a yellow flag that needs to be addressed). How you communicate and enforce them might, but the intrinsic value of your boundaries never should. So then, why do we talk about them like they would—hurt someone's feelings, that is? Why are we constantly apologizing or feeling like our wants, needs, and intrinsic responsibilities are something we should feel sorry for or be overly polite about?

There is a short clip from a television interview with the actress Elizabeth Olsen, where she says one of the greatest pieces of advice that her family ever gave her was that, "No is a full sentence… you can just say 'no'," (the off-camera show, 2021). The simplicity of this statement and belief cannot be denied, especially when it comes to our boundaries. While the actual phrasing of our boundaries might not include the word 'no', there is still some element of that word in the boundary (i.e., "I will not eat pork", "I do not kiss on the first date"). You do not have to soften your 'no's to make them more palatable for other people. In practical terms, what this means is that saying your boundary, without the unnecessary flamboyance or politeness, is enough.

Another crucial element of communicating your boundaries is ensuring that you state them in the appropriate time and place. You can be as polite, or as simplistic as you like when stating your boundaries, but if you do it at the wrong time and place, they will not be acknowledged, respected, or even considered the first go round.

Would you really listen to someone's boundaries at work if they just randomly stated: "I do not like going by that nickname anymore," during a team meeting? Most likely not. In fact, you may not even acknowledge what they said at first.

Communicating your boundaries is not just ensuring that you are simply and clearly stating your intent, or what you are or are not willing to be responsible for. It is also ensuring that you are doing it in an atmosphere of acknowledgement and receiving.

Receiving does not necessarily mean that the listener will honor the boundaries; it merely means that you have somehow ensured that the atmosphere is aware that you are going to speak and they need to noticeably acknowledge that you said something. Yes, that sounds awkward, but remember: People have the ability to not respect or remember your boundaries. Including when you have prepared the room to do so. Some boundaries—especially when it comes to consent, or you feeling or being unsafe—do not need an appropriate time or place.

Nonverbal Boundaries

These boundaries are a bit trickier, as they tend to forego the golden rule of this book which is to actually communicate (speak) your boundaries in a clear, precise manner in the correct context. So, nonverbal boundaries are something that should be used as a last resort, or perhaps as the first tiny step to beginning to communicate your boundaries.

Nonverbal boundaries are simply the act of you leaving, stopping, or not participating in something. Which is part of why they are a gray area of boundaries: They are not clear, precise or necessarily understood, acknowledged or perceived by those around you.

So why would someone use them? Simple: Nonverbal boundaries are the first step for yourself, on how you are going to take a stand for your actual boundaries.

No, this does not mean to create a post-board sign with your boundary written on it and walk around your office, home, or school. However, this could be you leaving the room quietly when you notice that gossip has taken over the conversation. The problem is that this type of action becomes a double-edged sword because while it allows you to begin getting comfortable being different in a crowd and to begin asserting your boundaries without yet vocalizing them, nonverbal boundaries have this precarious characteristic of appearing rude. If your friend suddenly was on their phone the entire time you and your friend group was having a conversation, which you viewed as harmless, would you think that was a boundary, or that they have checked out and no longer want to be there? Most likely the latter. Yet, for all you know, this could be your friend's silent way of signaling that they are uncomfortable.

So, while nonverbal boundaries may be necessary for either very strenuous situations (like tense work meetings), or something you intrinsically need to begin feeling more comfortable asserting yourself, use them sparingly and wisely. And, if need be, address them later on when you are finally able and comfortable to verbalize your boundaries.

Be Proactive

There are so many times in our lives where being proactive could save us a world of hurt, and boundaries are certainly one of them. How to be proactive with setting your boundaries is to start early. Setting boundaries early, as we learned, can require very good communication, but getting ahead of an unnecessary conflict can save you a lot of emotional time and energy (Castrillon, 2019).

A great example of being proactive with your boundaries is by mentioning them at the beginning of a new relationship, or not letting the little things slide. For example, letting the barista at your local coffee shop know that your drink is wrong is a great example. While how your coffee is made may not be an actual boundary, mentioning that your order is wrong, is respecting the boundary of your specific need at that moment.

This might seem a little patronizing, but bear with it for a moment. Part of the reason why you want to practice being proactive with your boundaries in the little things, is not just so that you become more assertive through practice, but also so that you are able to begin enforcing how your boundaries look to yourself.

If you are unaccustomed to setting boundaries, then being assertive—let alone proactive—are going to feel unnatural and almost like you are over-communicating to those around you. While it may be slightly true, for now, take that trait over not respecting or enforcing your boundaries, and simply begin to practice journaling or looking back at conversations in hindsight (at least an hour after you have had them) so that you can analyze if you over-communicated or if you were actually combating a boundary reactive fear or myth.

Practice, Practice, Practice

There is the old adage that "practice makes perfect", and in the case of boundaries, it is true. Being politely assertive is something that comes with practice. Even if you are naturally inclined to be assertive and very open about your wants, needs, and boundaries, practicing this assertiveness politely will never really steer you wrong.

In case you are wondering how you can practice being assertive, sadly, it is truly by just *being* assertive. This might sound too simple—because it is—but the real problem will come with you actually following through with it.

Helping you follow through with practicing your assertiveness for boundaries is going to be just as simple. Pick one or two small boundaries that consistently get crossed over (e.g., your coffee is not properly made, you let customer service workers be rude to you, or you let people around you be rude to you), and begin standing up for yourself.

Realistically, nothing else is going to help you combat your aversion to assertion, other than actually taking a breath and doing it.

That being said, your discomfort over that idea is completely understood. It is something that many of us deal with, but the only way to get through it, is to do it. Think of it as immersion therapy. It will only get better the more you do it and practice it.

Give Yourself Grace

The definition of 'grace' is the "disposition to or an act or instance of kindness, courtesy, or clemency, or a temporary exemption" (Merriam-Webster, n.d.). When it comes to how to give yourself grace, it means to acknowledge when you tried but failed, or when you failed and to not beat yourself up about it. This is especially true when it comes to being assertive with your boundaries.

There are going to be days where you are not going to be assertive on all of your boundaries, there are going to be days where you just cannot give the emotional energy to stand up or maintain them, and there are going to be days where you are being assertive or communicate your boundaries poorly. And you know what? It is okay.

We are all human, and we are all learning and figuring this out together, one day at a time. None of us are perfect, even though some try to give that impression. We are all going to have incidents, moments, or scenarios where we admit—even to ourselves—that that entire series of events could have gone better. Forgiving yourself, learning from it, and moving on with that knowledge is the key to getting yourself out of self-pity and into receiving your own grace.

Now, that is not a "get out of jail free card" for when you are too lazy, or not feeling like standing up for your boundaries or communicating with them properly. Because while you may be able to—and should—give yourself grace, the other parties may not be so inclined. And that is something you have to accept and be okay with, because if the tables were turned, would you forgive yourself?

Giving yourself grace is necessary, but not doing the work and then still asking and extending yourself grace—while it may happen on the occasional blue moon—is something you want, and should, avoid.

Do not take advantage of giving yourself grace to avoid doing the hard work; because you will not get farther on this journey and may do yourself more harm than good.

Combating Assertion Guilt

As mentioned before, guilt has this nasty way of attaching itself to almost anything and everything, including you beginning to assert your boundaries. So how do you combat the guilt that can come from your assertiveness?

By remembering the following:

You asserting and standing up for your boundaries, as long as it is done politely, is never something to feel guilty about. You are just as worthy of having your boundaries understood and respected as anyone else. You are just as worthy and capable of standing up for them as anyone else. Your boundaries are something you are able to be firm on, and you know yourself enough to know that your boundaries are worth fighting for.

Combating Your Weaknesses

First of all, let's get something clear: just because a few (or all) of these strategies are daunting does not mean that you cannot do this, or that you are intrinsically weak. It means that you have not had the ability to practice being assertive with your boundaries.

Which we will combat right here and now.

If any of these things are something you struggle with, take a moment to write them down and begin to ask yourself why they are hard for you. In your answers, do you notice anything to do with the boundary myths that were discussed? If so, you already have a good idea on how to begin rephrasing and combating those fears.

If standing up for yourself is difficult, it could be for many reasons: it could be something you are not confident in, something that has been ingrained into you from your culture, family, or society, you could be a people pleaser, or it could be because you are afraid that you will lose the relationships you assert boundaries in. Let's combat each of those worries individually.

Ingrained Behaviors

Unfortunately, boundaries are something that some of us learn from the cradle, while others are taught that it is a selfish pattern of behavior. If this is you, remember that boundaries are not a selfish behavior, and they are something that will be immensely helpful in your life and relationships going forward. Regrettably, what this also means is that you are going to have a time in re-learning how to think about your behaviors in order to ensure that you are confidently enforcing your boundaries. Good news is that you now have tools to reshape and combat the guilt you have been programmed to feel for sticking to your boundaries.

So, then, when it comes to combating the actual cause of your ingrained behaviors, begin by thinking where it originally came from. Was it a saying that your parents told you? An incident at school? Or how a friend or sibling scolded or even talked to you when you were younger? Identifying the underlying element of why you intrinsically believe that your boundaries are wrong will help you begin to find a strategy to fight them without feeling guilty.

This strategy that you come up with, as with everything in this chapter so far, is going to be relatively easy in theory, but incredibly difficult in practice. You are going to have to fight it with contradicting mantras.

For instance, if you were told as a child that your boundaries were something that you did not need to share, or were unnecessary, a simple way to combat that is to remind yourself that they *are* necessary, you *do* need them, and they *will* help you.

Again, easier said than done.

People Pleasing

Another reason why so many are unwilling to be assertive with their boundaries is because they are people pleasers.

Yes, you read that right.

People pleasing is actually a form of not respecting your own boundaries, because by the very definition, a people pleaser is someone whose emotional need to help others will come at the cost of their own (Merriam-Webster, 2022). Therefore, if you are a people pleaser, you are wired to ignore your own boundaries to please others, if that is what it will take.

Sounds a bit odd?

If your innermost desire or need is to please other people, sooner or later, your boundaries will upset someone—that is a sad fact of life. Which then means that you will be put in the awkward position of choosing between pleasing that person and honoring your boundaries, or discarding whatever boundary you have set to please the other person. While it is hoped that you would find a way to mediate between the two, but ultimately be willing to choose your boundaries over the other person, there is a very low chance of that happening if you have not already practiced foregoing your people pleasing tendencies.

Before closing this section off, two things should be noted. First, people pleasers are not bad people, they just have this bad tendency of foregoing their own needs for others when they really should not. If you are a people pleaser, do not worry, there is a whole chapter devoted to ensuring that you are firm and assertive with your boundaries in your life. Second, fighting people pleasing is hard, and that inner turmoil should never be belittled.

People pleasing is an ingrained habit that is sometimes done out of either a need or trauma, and either way, you are fighting what are most likely years-long habits in order to begin changing. That task is daunting, but you do not have to do it alone. That being said, if you are a people pleaser, or someone who has people pleasing tendencies, setting boundaries is going to be tricky for you, especially when it comes to boundaries and interpersonal relationships. Which means that you are going to have to work a bit harder than some others on your boundary journey.

A Few Tips

There is absolutely no way that you are going to be left hanging on what to do if you identify or are a people pleaser. In this segment a few things will be quickly mentioned to help you gain some perspective before discussing interpersonal relationships. Use this section wisely: Get your journal, write a few ideas down, take a few minutes to begin coming up with your own spin on the solutions that are presented here, and begin to enact them once you have a good handle on what to do. Fighting people pleasing will be hard, but in this instance, practice truly will make perfect.

First: Actually communicate your boundaries. It sounds odd, but communicating your needs and wants will help you begin to see who will respect your boundaries or not. And this is important as it will bring up our second tip (Tartakovsky, 2019).

Second: Only focus on the relationships that will nurture you (which you can identify by the people who will respect and encourage you setting healthy boundaries). As mentioned in the previous chapter, if someone does not respect your boundaries, even when you try to talk it through, then that is someone who is not necessarily going to encourage a healthy relationship with you—or even a healthy version of you. Those types of relationships will aim to take advantage of your people pleasing tendencies, which has a high likelihood of resulting in you being burned out and not getting what you need from that relationship (remember: relationships are all give and take, you cannot always be the giver).

Third: Begin to put yourself first. Often people pleasers put their identity and fulfillment of wants and needs onto/from/in other people. Not only is that dangerous for you as a person, but that is a blatant disrespect of your own boundaries; you are not accepting any responsibility for what you can or cannot handle, and are putting that entirely onto another person. While that may seem odd, since people pleasing tends to mean that you are doing everything possible to please someone else, remember the definition of a people pleaser: Their emotional wants and needs are intrinsically tied to fulfilling someone else's wants or needs (Merriam-Webster, 2022). That means their fulfillment will come from whatever they do to make someone else happy. While it is completely natural, healthy, and encouraged to feel happy when we make someone else happy, putting all of our ability to actually be happy off of someone else's reaction to our actions is not only convoluted and a lot of back and forth for some happiness, but it is also a good way to make someone else resentful of you over time, as well as ensure that you never actually know how to satisfy yourself on your own; neither of which are good or healthy places to be.

Again, if any of these things are you, or if you align with anything in this segment, do not worry or lose heart about your boundary journey. These three things were brought up so that you could begin to recognize and fight them in your life, not so that you could stop and lose heart. You can do it. You can set healthy boundaries and have healthy relationships; and it will actually feel so much better once you do.

Losing Relationships

The fear of losing relationships while asserting your boundaries deeply mirrors the myth of pushing people away, or those who feel that they are exempt from your boundaries—but with a bit of a twist. This twist is that you may be actually afraid of confrontation.

Wondering how we made that switch?

Confrontation is often seen as a companion to asserting your boundaries because so many people attempt to do it wrongly, or are pushed to their breaking point and then explode with their boundary communication. Both of these scenarios then present as a chaotic form of confrontation, which many people have a natural, or ingrained, aversion to. And if that natural aversion occurred when communicating a boundary, it makes sense as to why some people do not necessarily want to assert their boundaries.

If you are afraid to be assertive with your boundaries because you believe that will bring up a confrontation, answer the question of why this would bring up a confrontation. Is it because the other person has responded explosively to boundaries in the past? Is it because your boundary is in direct violation of theirs? Or is it because you are intrinsically standing up for yourself, and they are unaccustomed or do not want that?

How you answer these questions will then dictate how you should respond to the fear of losing that relationship. If it is because the person has exploded reactively in the past, begin to consider why that person exploded. Was it because of poor communication? Because that boundary violated or triggered them? Look at the scenario and begin to think of ways that you can present your boundary differently to avoid that outcome. There is a good likelihood that you may be able to avoid that type of response if you handle the situation properly

Small Note

If this is the type of person who is volatile and will never respond properly to your boundaries, seek professional help, and leave if you have too. Boundaries were meant to help heal, form, and maintain strong and healthy relationships. They were not meant for you to stay for duplicity, addition, or abuse of any kind.

Now, back to the second reaction, did someone react poorly to a boundary assertion because that boundary directly violated theirs? If so, then really consider the situation and why that boundary violated someone else's. Boundaries should never do that, unless someone is a manipulator, liar, or is using boundaries as an excuse to get away with poor behavior. Therefore, technically, healthy boundaries should mostly be in alignment with each other, and as long as you communicate (see how often this pops up?) properly, you should be good to go. However, if while you were analyzing that past scenario, you begin to notice that the other person's boundary is unhealthy—or that yours might be—seek professional help either from a counselor or safe person on how to address that specific person or boundary.

The third and final scenario is if the other person does not want, or is unaccustomed, to you asserting yourself. If someone does not want you to assert yourself, then leave. They will not be a healthy addition to your boundary journey and will definitely not be a safe person to support and guide you. Again, please note: This only applies if your boundaries are healthy and respectful of yourself and others, and if you have tried to assert yourself respectfully in the past.

Now, if someone is unaccustomed to you asserting yourself and has reacted poorly, consider giving them grace and talking about it either on your own, or with a safe person, therapist, or mediator. That reaction may require figuring out how to make sure that your boundaries are heard while they work through their own fears and boundaries. Thankfully, you can both figure out how to combat those together.

Journaling

Now that you know what boundaries are, what boundaries look like, and how to be assertive and confident in your boundaries without guilt, it is time to practically take a few moments to think through which strategy will work best for you.

In all honesty, a combination of everything that has been mentioned would be ideal, but some may take longer or more practice than others—and that is okay. Figuring out how you personally are going to be assertive is not an immediate thought or action; it is you testing out different things, confronting certain fears or boundary myths, as well as constantly checking yourself to ensure that you are being assertive without being rude.

So, with that in mind, take a few moments to pick the assertive strategies you naturally excel at, as well as the ones that scare you, or you are not strong at. Begin to make a plan on how to be stronger in all of the assertive strategies. A good way to start is by picking one and attempting it the next time you need to communicate your boundaries.

Do not forget to give yourself grace while practicing. You may not get it right the first time, and that is okay. You can do this.

CHAPTER 4

Setting Boundaries in Relationships

Now that we have gone over how to be assertive with your boundaries, it is time to look at each area of your life to see exactly why you need to set boundaries and how you can start. In this chapter we will discuss how to see where these areas of your life do, or do not, have boundaries, and where to go from there.

Extenuating Circumstances

As mentioned previously, there are times where your boundaries are going to encounter extenuating circumstances. These specifically refer to areas where you are not safe, in personal danger, in relationship with an extremely unsafe person (like addicts, serial liars, psychopaths, or sociopaths), or in certain life phases such as with newborns or elderly/dementia patients, where boundaries need extra steps.

If you are in an unsafe relationship or scenario, know this right now: No boundary is going to save you.

Addicts, serial liars, manipulators, psychopaths or sociopaths will never respect your boundaries, and you should not continue to put yourself at risk. Understanding and setting your boundaries will help you going forward once you exit that relationship, but for the immediate future: Get out. Find a safe person who will help you get away to a safe place where you can gain perspective.

If you are in one of those strange life phases where your boundaries will honestly not be a lot of help with one particular relationship (such as a newborn, dementia or specific elderly relatives/people you know), then really the best way through it is to stick up for your boundaries the best way you can (this is specifically for the elderly or dementia patients), but extend a lot of grace to the situation.

Consider this example: Michelle's grandmother has extreme bipolar disorder, as well as heavy depression, which has made her incredibly volatile and emotionally unstable over the years. The family had developed methods to cope, but now the grandmother has developed terminal breast cancer, and the family has been given six months. Michelle, while aware and firm on her boundaries, was one of the main care-givers during this time. While she did not tolerate verbal abuse from her grandmother, she also did not correct every little thing, or pay attention when her grandmother had just taken her heavy pain medication.

While this example is incredibly depressing, it perfectly showcases a time in some people's lives where their boundaries are still important, but there is this awful give and take on when to enforce them, versus when to let things go. In the case of Michelle, this example showcases that as one of her grandmother's main caretakers for the limited end of the grandmother's life, Michelle recognized that her boundaries were important and needed to be honored; but her grandmother also needed help and would not always entirely be herself due to medication and the effects of specific treatment.

Remember the previous chapter on when it was appropriate to enforce your boundaries? Enforcing them to a patient who is incredibly high off of painkillers, or incredibly sick and tired from serious medical treatment, is one of those times.

Small Note

Now, this is not to say that Michelle would let her grandmother verbally abuse her, or let her grandmother's mental conditions get in the way of how her grandmother constantly treated her. However, there is also the fine line of insisting that an unhealthy person (in this case due to the bad mental health of a dying patient) maintain healthy mindsets versus incredibly stressful and depressing circumstances.

The problem with any extenuating circumstances which have been mentioned is that they are incredibly special and specific to you, your boundaries, and the situation. For instance, some people might be in Michelle's shoes, but need their boundaries to be more respected, even during that time, due to previous traumas of their past. That is completely okay. Because these types of situations are so specific, if you are unsure or not able to monitor yourself and what your boundaries can or cannot handle, use a safe person or therapist who can help guide you. Not because you are unable to do it yourself, but because these scenarios are inherently stressful and having a third, neutral opinion might help you gain a better perspective and figure out what to do.

Now, going back to relatively normal relationships and the boundaries needed in those relationships. This section will be divided into the main elements of your life (family, friends, work, and romantic relationships). Each section will discuss how these boundaries work, and give examples on what communicating/using them may look like.

These examples specifically cover each area (roughly) of your life for several reasons: First, it will help you to really see and debunk any of the previous boundary myths you may think you are unconsciously enacting, but are unsure of. Second, while boundaries are something that encompass and transcend every part of your life, the enactment and firm way to uphold those boundaries may be slightly different depending on who you are with and the situation. Third, once you begin to see how a simple boundary, like "I do not like hugging people", can transcend and morph between the different areas of your life, you will be able to be more consistent when enforcing your boundaries—while simultaneously beginning to ensure that your boundaries are fluid enough to stay firm to what they are, but adapt to different situations and relationships.

Setting Boundaries With Family Members

When it comes to families there is one relationship where boundaries become a bit of a sore spot, and that is with authority figures and parents. While this section will also cover siblings, parental and authority figures will definitely consist of the lion's share for one very important reason: the power dynamic shifts throughout the course of our lives, and so too, will our boundaries and how the respect for those boundaries is enacted.

Parents and Authority Figures

Enacting and consistently enforcing boundaries with parents or authority figures can become a mental minefield of navigating either self-induced, or enforced guilt and feelings of shame and/or selfishness, along with just trying to gain a basic understanding of respect versus overstepping boundaries. And the fluidity of the relationship between parents and children in regards to power dynamics and boundaries does not help the situation.

What this power shift is alluding to is the growth of the children and how boundaries and responsibilities shift as we grow. When we were younger, or minors, the power lay mostly with the adults. Therefore, while boundaries were hopefully still in existence, certain wants and needs, or extensions of boundaries, were not always as debatable. In comparison, as adults, our boundaries should be respected and acknowledged; yet how that actually looks becomes a bit of a foggy mess that can cause confusion, angst, and a lot of miscommunication.

Please Note

The above statement has absolutely nothing to do with fundamental human right-based boundaries such as: physical, sexual, and emotional safety, nourishment, or simple lack of abuse.

If any of those things occurred—or are occurring—get professional help. This could be a therapist, a friend or other authority figure who you trust, or authority figures in your community who will believe and listen to you.

If this happened to you, first of all: That is awful, and you did absolutely nothing to deserve it. Second, your boundaries will come with heavily related traumas, and you should seek professional help (such as a therapist or counselor) when you begin to address and resolve the boundaries that have been broken. While this book will help you, it will not cover traumatic events or triggers specifically (they will only be mentioned), and that type of help should honestly be reserved for professionals.

Changing Boundaries

Now, back to authority figures and boundaries. As previously mentioned, these types of boundaries tend to morph and change when power dynamics shift, or, as we grow. Take body modifications, like tattoos or piercings, for example. As a minor (depending on where you live) there is most likely an age limit on when you can get these things done without the consent of an adult/authority figure who is a predominant guardian. However, as we get older, those types of enforcements no longer exist. Once you come of age, you can get any type of modification you want. The problem (and why this whole section is being written) then becomes the personal boundaries of living situations, parents, you, the power shift of your home, etc. Handling and figuring out how those boundaries work are honestly a tumultuous and incredibly sensitive time, which is why reading and understanding the different phases from both perspectives (children and parents) is going to be addressed.

Because this section is large, it will be parsed into multiple views to discuss the various angles.

First, we will discuss younger boundaries, where you as the reader will be able to gain insight on how certain boundaries may or may not have been respected from your childhood. Then we will move onto older boundaries which will roughly be teenage to young adult years. This section will specifically discuss how certain power shifts will affect your boundaries, and how to deal with that. Each of these sections will then have their own perspective section for parents of that age group.

The goal of parsing these sections up in such a way is to help you gain perspective on your childhood and possibly why your parents may have handled things in a certain way, or, conversely, to see what healthy boundaries when you are a young child or teenager with healthy boundary respecting parents looks like—with the hindsight of being an adult who is now armed with a good foundation of knowledge on boundaries. Additionally, with the added sections of parental perspectives, you will hopefully be able to glean not only an understanding of what parents go through, but be able to see the vast difference between fully formed and functioning adult boundaries versus children's boundaries, and how your own have morphed over time.

Understanding how your boundaries have changed will accomplish two things. First, it will help you begin to realize that even now your boundaries have the ability to be fluid as life changes. Second, it will help you begin to really see how certain boundaries you may have thought were being disrespected by your parents, most probably were not. Or, on the very awful chance that they were, confirm your suspicions.

Younger Boundaries

When we are younger, our parents hold the majority of power over our lives. Honestly, it sounds harsh, but this is most likely for the best (if you are beginning to get annoyed, do not worry, just keep reading). Our parents or authority figures have years of real-life world experience, meaning that they most likely (sadly, not always) are able to use that wisdom to help us grow.

For instance, most parents or authority figures know that you should not wear shorts when it is snowing outside, yet as a three-year-old, that logic may not be understandable or even fully formed. Which is where boundaries come in. Parents have the authority and boundary knowledge to ensure that those who are of primary school age or younger cannot do those types of things, or put themselves into dangerous or harmful situations.

However, that type of authority also comes with heavy responsibility. It is hoped that while the authority figures have this type of power/dominance of their own, that they will be able to teach you responsibility and wise decision making to the point where you will be able to function and continue to grow on your own, once this balance in power begins to shift (the next section).

What this means is that when we are younger, our boundaries should still be respected, but in comparison to older boundaries, younger boundaries are more so taught and felt, than cognitively perceived. Four year olds know perfectly well what they will or will not tolerate or accept, but they may not be completely able to tell you why. Most parents, when you look at them closely, seem to intrinsically (or they have done a lot of book reading on the subject, hopefully) understand which boundary is intrinsic to their child, versus ones that may have to be walked through to either see why their logic is wrong, or to help them better define what their boundary actually is.

So what does this mean for you, a fully grown and mainly functioning adult? Well, sometimes as young children we predominantly feel like our boundaries were wronged, but are unable to fully explain why. And unfortunately, there are some cases where that could be true. If you believe this is you, then it is strongly recommended that you find professional help to begin working through that trauma. However, for most of us that may not be the case. Think back to those moments where you felt severely wronged as a young child, and then begin to look at it through the eyes of your now boundary-knowing brain. Were your boundaries being disrespected, or did your parents or authority figures just not explain their reasoning behind it well?

Consider this example:

Even though it happened decades ago, there is still a small part of you that is upset (even though you understand that you need to let it go, because it was years ago) that your parents seemed to always make you share your toys, but your cousin—to your knowledge—was never made to, either.

Put into adult perspective, most of us are also aware that these types of annoyances are irrational and not relevant anymore. However, that annoyance has a teeny, tiny, kernel of truth/acceptance to it, because it signifies that we were unable to let go of a transgression that happened to us. In this instance, it was that you were made to share, while your equal was not. Therefore, the very boundary of equality and respect—something many of us know from an early age—was, in our minds, deeply wronged. However, as adults, we are able to recognize that we did not know the other side of that story. Perhaps your cousin was forced to share and you do not remember it, or they lied about it. Whatever the reason, understanding why we are still angry over the transgression of boundaries from our childhood years will be fundamental knowledge in understanding how certain frustrations may be playing out now—especially when it comes to enacting and enforcing healthy boundaries with people you may already have a decades long grudge against.

Parents of Younger Boundaries

On the other hand, setting boundaries as a parent can be just as daunting, because now you are responsible for ensuring that this little human is somehow a functioning adult with hopefully relatively healthy boundaries. And, depending on the age, your ability to get the child to understand boundaries is going to be an uphill battle.

Thankfully children's boundaries develop very quickly; and it is the job of the parents to not only honor those boundaries, but help if they are a bit out of alignment. For instance, going back to the shorts and snow example. What if the child was now thirteen, instead of four? Suddenly the parent is faced with a difficult choice of playing the parental card of "you still cannot wear that," versus letting them test those waters to learn the lesson and figure out if that boundary was worth fighting for.

Now, that is a lot of moving factors for one child. Imagine two or three. Now imagine they are all growing and reaching new milestones roughly every couple months or every year, depending on the age. Hopefully, you are beginning to get the idea of how parents struggle to sometimes understand and recognize every single boundary that is thrown their way.

Again, that is in no way an excuse for parents who deliberately ignore their child's boundaries; and that is certainly not saying that any type of abuse or neglect (physical, emotional, addiction, duplicity, etc.) are okay on any level.

What this does mean is that some of us as adults specifically remember a time when our firm and emphatic 'no' based boundary was not respected, and while that memory may still bring up intense feelings of frustration, hurt, or anger, you may also be getting an inkling as to why that boundary was ignored.

If you are a parent with young children, then here is a great rule of thumb: Teaching them about responsibility, if done right, will never go wrong. The more young children are responsible (as long as it is age appropriate, like cleaning their toys), will help them begin to understand the intrinsic relationship between their boundaries and the responsibilities that go with it.

That does not mean to give your child more than they can handle, or that you should make everything about responsibility. Again, it is all about balance.

Boundaries of Adult Children

Compared to small children, teenagers and adult children (essentially anyone in their twenties and up) possess fully formed and functioning boundaries; and it is at this stage that the power dynamic begins to stir up friction. Remember the teenage years? Or perhaps you are a teenager now. It might very well feel like your parents are not respecting your boundaries. And, sadly, for some of you, they might not be.

However, on the small chance that your parents might be, or did, respect your boundaries, begin to think about the reasons why certain things were denied. For instance, that age-old adage of "not under my roof!", was a pretty common one a couple of years ago. And, while it may be irksome, while it may be annoying, that is a boundary parents and authority figures are more than allowed to have. And ones that should be respected as long as they are reasonable.

Going back a few examples, it is perfectly reasonable (but can one hundred percent totally suck) that your parents have a rule or boundary where you are not allowed to get any new body modifications while living under their roof. Which is also why so many people get them the minute they move out during their university years. Respecting that boundary of your parents is your duty because: they are the adult, it is their house, and for your boundaries to be respected, you have to respect theirs.

And while it is really painful on a certain level to say this: You wanting a body modification (or something like that) is not a boundary violation. However, at the same time, your parents putting restrictive boundaries on you not only causes friction, but can also create many gray areas of how to handle boundaries. For instance, if you are twenty one and your parents are still not allowing body modifications in their home, while it is their right to have that rule in their house, it also becomes awkward because you are twenty one, and that type of boundary is a bit restrictive for your age.

You can always combat that by attempting to have a sit-down communication with your parents, or by moving out. Again, their house, their rules; which is perfectly respectable. Especially since body modifications are not a fundamental human right.

Sounds messy, right?

As an adult child, begin to think about your boundaries and why they are important to you. For instance, using the body modification example, the modification is not the boundary, but having your parents respect your ability to make wise choices might be. Confronting your parents has to be done with respect and awareness of the bigger picture. Simply going up to them and saying, "I am an adult and can do what I want!" will get you nowhere, and will just result in a large fight or make further progress a lot harder.

What Those Boundaries Look Like

Regardless as to your living situation, here are a few things you can do to begin implementing healthy boundaries with your parents as an adult child.

First: You can assemble the boundaries—and their enactments—you want respected. Take a good long look to see if they deliberately violate any of your parents own boundaries, such as ingrained house rules, or specific responsibilities or values they personally have. If your boundaries violate theirs, or are specifically going against their beliefs, you may have to re-think either your living situation before discussing your boundaries with them, or, ensure that you walk them through your logic to get to a middle ground of mutual understanding and respect.

Second: Be assertive, but compassionate and open to communicating or answering questions they might have. It might sound silly, but you will always be your parents/guardians child, so when you confront them with very adult-like boundaries, they may intrinsically panic. And you may have to be the bigger person and help walk them through what this will look like, and how you will ensure your safety. Being open to communicating and answering questions will go a long way in not only easing their fears, but beginning the process of open communication and understanding.

Third: you need to know the limits. There are going to be some boundaries—which will still need to be stated—that might truly need some conditioning for your parents or authority figures to begin understanding or accepting them. This is where the grace that was previously talked about, comes in. For most of us, our parents want us to live a happy, thriving and successful life. Unfortunately, a lot of our conflicts come through the clashing of how they view that life versus how we intend to live it. Establishing and maintaining open communication about these things will go a long way in being able to respect your own boundaries and theirs. Sometimes you, or your parents/authority figures, will need to take a step back to gain clarity and space. This is natural and healthy, and while it may freak some people out due to personality, conflict resolution, or past traumas, do not rush this process. Forcing someone to accept your boundaries by constantly harassing them through the guise of open communication is not fair, and a good way to breed resentment. On the same side, you being able to tell your parents you need some space to think things through and gather your thoughts alerts them to the fact that not only have you matured enough to understand when you need time to think; it will also give you the ability to regroup and reconfigure how you are going to ensure that this boundary is respected.

As Parents

Alright, so many things were said to the adult children. Now it is time for the parents. As parents, there are going to be many times when your children will want a certain thing that you wish they did not—such as those body modifications, or less than ideal living situations. However, there are several things to remember: the first is that if they are legally of age, there is not a lot you can do if it is not under your roof. And no, you cannot keep them under your roof if they do not want to stay.

What this also means is that, just like your child, you still have a right to your own boundaries and house rules. Do not let your child sway you otherwise, unless it is something you truly believe needs to be swayed.

However, there is another aspect of setting boundaries with adult children that needs to be discussed: implementing stronger boundaries if your adult child is taking advantage of you. Before you get up in arms saying, "They are my child, they can't take advantage of me!" begin to think about their life circumstances, what you are currently doing, and how involved in their lives you actually are. It is one thing if your child is a student and you are occasionally helping financially because that was either the deal, or they are struggling. What is really being discussed here, are the adult children who are still coddled like a child. This is going to hurt to hear, but if that is you and your child, you are enabling them to live an irresponsible life.

While that statement might seem a bit heavy-handed, remember, you are the parent. Meaning no one knows the boundaries and expectations in play better than you. Once you realize the value of your own boundaries, you can start to see the difference between if they actually need help, versus them just wanting to be lazy and you're just making life too easy for them. It might be time for them to learn some hard truths.

So how do you set those boundaries?

According to Allison Bottke, there are several easy steps to begin setting your own boundaries to ensure that both you and your child are living a boundary-healthy life: stop swooping in, gather a support group, immediately stop excuses, implement your own boundaries and respect them, trust your instincts (you have raised them this long, it is time to see if that gut instinct is still in tact) and yield to the understanding that you fixing everything will not ensure your child's long-term success, (Bottke, 2022/2019).

Setting Boundaries With Siblings

Alright, so with parental and authority figures out of the way, it is time to consider boundaries with siblings. Similar to parental/authority figures, your siblings live with you for a certain period of your life, meaning that they most likely know, or have a good idea, of what your boundaries already are. The problem then, is because your sibling intrinsically knows your boundaries—but does not know the specifics since they most likely have not been told what the boundary actually is—things can get lost in translation and the enactment of understanding. But, let's not forget that this is discussing siblings. Which means that miscommunication and misunderstandings run high, as well as quick and easy tempers, ignorance, and the deliberate choice of ignorance in some situations.

Thankfully, enforcing and beginning to establish boundaries with your siblings, like with your parents, boils down to several key habits that you are already aware of. Clearly communicating your boundaries, respecting your own boundaries, and having fail-safe plans in place for when your sibling does not respect your boundaries (starting a fight or confrontation does not count).

Now, another thing that could be useful in regards to siblings could be finding a safe person to be your mediator when tempers run, so high that there is no way you would be able to clearly communicate through it.

Before closing off the family section there is a tiny caveat that should be discussed: Just because they are your family does not mean that they should be given the extension of grace constantly when they willingly choose to ignore or not recognize your boundaries. The saying "blood is thicker than water" should not extend towards your personal safety, or your mental, physical or spiritual well-being. All of which are defined, communicated, and enforced through the enactment and respect of your boundaries.

With Friends

Boundaries with friends arc pretty similar to boundaries with siblings, except with one crucial difference: Your friends may not know you as well as your siblings, because they most likely have not lived with you, or known you for that long. Which then means that you have to really up your communication game to ensure that your friends respect your boundaries. And that means being prepared to have uncomfortable talks, if necessary.

For instance, say you have two friends: James and Mike. You have known them for a few years and they have always pushed you outside of your comfort zone, but in good ways. They encouraged you when you were scared, but also challenged you to do things you would not normally do. When you tell them your limits, they respect them, and help you either work through them (if it is a fear-based problem you want to confront), or help you find solutions if it is something you are unwilling to change. They listen to you when you say that it is a hard limit and you are uncomfortable. And they also ask you questions on when you want to be pushed, and when you do not.

Notice how James and Mike ensured that communication was the foundation for how they respect your boundaries, as well as encouraged you to do things you were scared to do (remember the myth of saying no). This type of open communication and respect of boundaries is what you should strive for in your friendships and boundaries.

Setting Boundaries in Romantic Relationships

Boundaries in romantic relationships are both easy and difficult. They are easy because they are discussed more frequently, and more people are willing to put effort into maintaining those types of boundaries. They are also difficult because they involve being vulnerable with someone you most likely want to keep in your life, but that vulnerability comes at the cost of baring your soul and being willing to communicate about it. On top of that, there is the added problem of what was discussed in the first chapter: your happiness, wants, and needs, are not necessarily your partners' full-time job. Yes, they should be aiming to make you happy and to meet your wants and needs, but they are not solely responsible for them. You are.

Remember: Your boundaries are what *you* are responsible for. So, if one of your wants in the relationship is to have good communication, it is not fair—or right—for you to expect that of your partner, but then you yourself do not engage or communicate regularly.

So then, how do you ensure that your wants and needs are taken care of, while your boundaries are respected? Easy. Communicate with your partner, and be responsible (Gilles, n.d.). Sounds too good to be true, right? Well, you are not entirely wrong. Communicating with your partner—as many probably know—takes a lot of effort. But it is honestly worth the effort. Proper communication eliminates any guess work on your end as you have established that it is okay for you to ask questions and validate what you believe they are thinking or feeling in a given scenario (with the footnote that you are okay to be wrong and to be gently corrected).

Additionally, taking responsibility will lift a huge weight off of the pressure of a relationship, as well as the additional pressure of maintaining boundaries in a relationship, because you are straight up owning your responsibilities in the relationship (like your choices, your emotions, and your actions). Being proactive and taking ownership will save you numerous fights as well as begin to establish the enactment of healthy boundaries.

At Work

Depending on where you work, boundaries at work may not be an issue at all. Or perhaps it is one of the more impossible sections of this book. Part of the reason why boundaries at work seem so impossible is because we believe that if something is given to us, we have to jump immediately to solve or accomplish that task, leading to long days, few moments of rest, and a feeling like we are drowning under the corporate pile of never-ending paperwork and training seminars.

But it does not have to be that way.

Thankfully, most companies actually do have systems in place (or they are putting them in place) to help you build better boundaries, except it is not phrased that way. Often, when confronting work boundaries—or the lack thereof —the key word that is used is 'burnout', because the results are the same. Having no boundaries at work results in you taking on so much more than you can handle, which leads to you being burned out. One of the best solutions to burnout is to begin communicating your boundaries clearly and being proactive before things and projects escalate out of control.

However, there are several things that go into this boundary implementation plan, a lot of which include you doing some deep soul-searching.

Work Journaling

Alright, so, first off, take a moment with your journal and begin to ask yourself the following hard questions:

What am I actually responsible for in this position? What do I feel responsible for?

Then, really sit there and begin to think about how different those two lists are (if they are not, but you are still feeling like your boundaries are not being respected at work, do not worry, we will get there).

Often, when identifying where our boundaries are going awry in places like the workplace, we have to begin separating what we are actually responsible for, versus what we think we are being asked to accomplish; the overstepping of our boundaries are often found in the differences between those lists.

If you notice a difference, set up a meeting with your boss and begin to discuss that difference specifically. For that meeting you should not only have those two lists, but also have what you make a priority for your role (which should include your understanding of the role so far). Additionally, go into that meeting being prepared to negotiate your tasks and what will be required of you, but ensure that it is honestly what you can handle in a workday.

Now, if you do not notice that type of discrepancy (or even if you do), begin to look at the reasons why you might be feeling overwhelmed, specifically by looking at your day and journaling/writing down what is causing you stress and anxiety. Is it because your coworkers take up too much of your time? Is it because your inbox gets way too full? Is it because you need help but do not want to ask? When working on a team with multiple people, being sure of your boundaries is a key practice to success, but somewhere along the line, we forgot that boundaries include being okay to ask for help, or referring to other people, or even—gasp—delegating when we actually cannot complete something.

Somehow, modern society has taken the concept of pushing ourselves to the limit to pushing ourselves closer to the brink of insanity, rather than ensuring that we, and others, actually excel. Confused about how the two paragraphs link up? Let's walk it through from the beginning. Your boundaries are what you can or cannot handle and what you will or will not be responsible for. And somewhere along the line, you forgot to ensure that those boundaries were respected at work because you are now feeling overwhelmed, overworked, and probably underappreciated and over stressed. So, then, where are those boundaries going wrong?

They are either going wrong in your lack of communicating your boundaries or maintaining them, your lack of refusal to delegate your workload to honor your boundaries and your lack or inability to say no and set limits. As mentioned multiple times throughout this book: Saying no, as long as it is not refusing your actual job or what is expected of you, is not a bad thing. And if you have somehow worked yourself into a corner where you have taken on too much and cannot necessarily back out easily, schedule a talk with your manager and be honest. Most managers (again, not all, this would be something that you would know better) appreciate honesty. If you admit you made a mistake, but are able to show your proactivity by bringing a list of how you will not do this again, admitting you made a mistake should technically not be a black mark on your record within that company.

Online

This section is a little new, but in our increasingly technological-based world it is very important to begin to figure out what your boundaries will be with any type of media. These boundaries specifically involve the question of: what you will or will not share and tolerate online.

For instance, will it be okay for you to have a public account and invite anyone and everyone to see, like, and comment on your photos? Including the trolls? Additionally, are you being appropriate for the platform and the type of account you have created? Influencers aside, it is rarely seen as appropriate to overshare your personal life on a business account, yet so many people do it. Which results in blurred boundaries and a poor enactment of what your responsibilities—for a professional account—are.

To set good online boundaries, seriously consider the platform and account. Think about what you want those things to represent, and which aspect of your life they align with. Create several different accounts if that is what it takes, but ensure that your boundaries are firm and well thought out here, because what goes online will never go away (Castrillon, 2019).

Journaling

That was a lot of information, so again, feel free to re-read this chapter and highlight or take notes on anything you specifically want to focus on going forward.

Before going forward, really look at each life relationship and begin to plot out where certain relationships of yours could use with some boundary strengthening. Look at the examples and strategies given and use those to create your own plan.

Chapter 5

Life With Boundaries

While it sounds repetitive, it cannot be overstated: Life with boundaries is so much simpler and easier to deal with.

Hopefully by now you have a pretty good idea of what your boundaries are, how you are going to enforce them, where you are lacking boundaries, and how you are going to begin re-enforcing them.

However, before completely ending the talk on boundaries, we still have to consider what your life will look like with them, specifically through a few things that you have been promised would be discussed and have not been yet. These areas include how to handle those who are going to ignore your boundaries and what your duty is going forward.

Confronting the Ignorant

Sadly, there will still be people who ignore your boundaries. And there is not much you can do about it. If the relationship is important to you, you can try to communicate with them, get a mediator or therapist to join those conversations, and come up with game plans together. But at the end of the day, if they do not put in the effort to respect your boundaries, you may have to be okay with distancing yourself from that relationship.

While it sounds harsh, there is nothing worse for you—especially right now—than being close to someone who is not going to respect your boundaries. Embarking on this journey is going to be hard, and it is going to require so much consistency that having a large cheer squad to help you through it is honestly almost a requirement. Since this journey is going to be that hard (anything that requires consistency does), having even one close negative influence might be enough to persuade you to stop.

Do not let that happen. You have done so much of the ground work already, do not stop now.

If that was not enough to sway you, consider this: The people who are ignoring your boundaries are probably one of the main reasons (as long as you are communicating and doing the groundwork discussed so far) you may feel like your boundaries are not being met. Most people are highly aware of when their boundaries are not being met, but many will give their relationships the benefit of the doubt—as they should. Perhaps you were not clear enough, perhaps they misunderstood, perhaps they forgot. All of these potential circumstances are more than possible, but it is your duty to figure out if they are reality.

If they are not, then not only is that relationship deliberately ignoring something you need, but you have already picked up on it. And if you have already picked up on it and are noticing the negative effects of that, why are you fighting to stay?

What Goes Around Comes Around

Once more: Your boundaries are yours alone, and they deserve respect.

However, if you expect other people to respect your boundaries, you have to reciprocate. It is incredibly selfish of you to expect everyone else to know, remember, and respect your boundaries while you completely walk all over someone else's.

Boundaries are built on communication, yes, but also on mutual respect.

Conclusion

And with that, we have reached the end of our book on boundaries. Hopefully you are more than prepared and eager to continue on your boundary journey. As you continue, remember several things:

- It will be hard, but worth it.
- You need to be consistent.
- Communication is key.
- The myths are called 'myths' for a reason.
- You are worthy of your boundaries being respected in every relationship you come across.
- Boundaries work on a reciprocal rule.

If you ever feel like this journey is too much for you, reach out to a safe person. It is completely okay if you cannot do this alone. Even if you need a cheering squad, ask someone for it, and know that so many people are cheering you on to begin your healthy boundary journey.

Thank You

Before you leave, I'd just like to say, thank you so much for purchasing my book.

I spent many days and nights working on this book so I could finally put this in your hands.

So, before you leave, I'd like to ask you a small favor.

Would you please consider posting a review on the platform? Your reviews are one of the best ways to support indie authors like me, and every review counts.

Your feedback will allow me to continue writing books just like this one, so let me know if you enjoyed it and why. I read every review and I would love to hear from you. Simply visit the link below to leave a review.

www.ingramcontent.com/pod-product-compliance
Lightning Source LLC
Chambersburg PA
CBHW081327120626
46546CB00011B/3255
9781959750123